Business
in Politics

Business in Politics

Campaign Strategies of Corporate Political Action Committees

Edward Handler
John R. Mulkern
Babson College

LexingtonBooks
D.C. Heath and Company
Lexington, Massachusetts
Toronto

Library of Congress Cataloging in Publication Data

Handler, Edward.
  Business in politics.

  Bibliography: p.
  Includes index.
  1. Business and politics—United States. 2. Corporations—United States—
Political activity. 3. Political action committees—United States. 4. United
States—Politics and government—1977-1981. I. Mulkern, John R. II. Title.
JK467.H27   1982   322'.3   81-48560
ISBN 0-669-05428-3   AACR2

Copyright © 1982 by D.C. Heath and Company

Published simultaneously in Canada

Printed in the United States of America

International Standard Book Number: 0-669-05428-3

Library of Congress Catalog Card Number: 81-48560

For Rita and Shirley

Contents

List of Tables

Acknowledgments

It is a pleasure to acknowledge the debts accumulated in preparing this study. The Board of Research at Babson College provided indispensable funding without which the extensive interviewing that is the hallmark of the research design could not have been undertaken. The board's assistance made possible some release from teaching at a critical stage of the writing. We are particularly obligated to the late Walter H. Carpenter without whose enthusiastic support it is unlikely that the study could have been launched. As vice-president for academic affairs and chairman of the Board of Research, he opened doors for others. We know the pleasure he would have taken in seeing this work come to publication.

Whatever value this study possesses is heavily dependent on the distinctiveness of its data base. No other researchers, to our knowledge, have interviewed PAC practitioners so widely. Interviews with seventy-one officers of PACs sponsored by major corporations were conducted. Before we began arranging the interviews, we were warned that necessary access and candor would not be forthcoming from the corporate world. This was not, in fact, our experience. To the contrary, PAC executives seemed eager to talk to academic scholars and to present their points of view, so long as there was reasonable assurance of necessary objectivity, detachment, and basic fairness in reporting what they said. We are grateful to these executives, who gave generously of their time, talked freely about their experiences, and shared data about their operations. They did so on the condition that necessary confidentiality and anonymity be maintained. We have tried scrupulously to respect that condition in the pages that follow. However important the data provided by PAC officers, our conclusions and interpretations are our own, and we bear entire responsibility for them.

All researchers on campaign finance can call upon the immense information resources that are available in the public-records office of the Federal Election Commission (FEC). This is one of the fringe benefits for scholarship that results from the reporting-and-disclosure requirements of the Federal Election Campaign Act provided by Congress. Craig Brightup of the staff of the FEC was unfailingly helpful in providing guidance and access to these resources.

At an early stage of the work we had the benefit of invaluable discussions with a number of highly knowledgable individuals representing a variety of viewpoints about the corporate-PAC phenomenon. They include: Stevenson Walker, then of the Public Affairs Council; Bernadette Budde, director of political education, Business-Industry Political Action Committee (BIPAC); Michael Malbin, resident scholar at the American Enterprise Institute for Public Policy Research; Fred Radewagen and John Kochevar,

National Chamber Alliance for Politics; Victor Kamber, then of the AFL-CIO; David Cohen, then president of Common Cause; Jeb Carney, Republican National Committee; Kenneth Feltman and David Landsidle, National Association of Manufacturers; David Moulton, Congress Watch; Paul Weyrich, Committee for Survival of a Free Congress; and Robert E. Moss, then general counsel, Committee on House Administration. Participating in these discussions was our colleague, Lawrence Godtfredsen, who also conducted over twenty of the interviews with PAC officers and helped in the preliminary analysis of the data.

Some of the material presented in this book originally appeared in "Diversity and Cohesion in Corporate Political Behavior: A Micro-Analysis of the Campaign Contribution Strategies of Corporate Political Action Committees," *Proceedings of the Academy of Management 1980*, and in "Corporate PACs as Fundraisers," *California Management Review* (Spring 1981).

Anne Oliveri, Board of Research secretary, did an outstanding job typing the manuscript.

1 Introduction

For students of interest-group politics, one of the more noteworthy phenomena of the 1970s has been the emergence and proliferation of corporate political-action committees (PACs) as a result of the passage of the Federal Election Campaign Act of 1971 and subsequent amendments in 1974 and 1976. By December 1974, eighty-nine corporate PACs had registered with the Federal Election Commission (FEC); by July 1981 the figure had risen to 1,251, a fourteenfold expansion in less than seven years.[1] Congress has provided a new opportunity for corporate managers to enter the political arena and to make campaign contributions to candidates, although corporations themselves remain forbidden, as they have been since 1907 at the federal level, to make direct campaign contributions from the corporate treasury in support of candidates.

The main provisions of the legislation of the 1970s as they relate to corporate PACs may be summarized as follows: Corporations may set up separate, segregated funds and political committees to administer them. These committees may collect money and disburse it on behalf of candidates. They may solicit stockholders, administrative, executive, and professional employees at any time. They may also solicit rank-and-file employees twice a year by mail. Congress made an effort to safeguard the principle of voluntarism in giving. Those who are solicited must be informed of their right not to contribute without punishment or reprisal. They must also be provided with a statement of the purpose for which accumulated funds will be expended. The committee that manages the fund may choose the candidates to whom campaign contributions are to be made. However, some committees permit contributors to earmark their contributions for designated candidates. The expenses of solicitation and other costs of administration may be defrayed by the corporation.

There are elaborate and detailed reporting-and-disclosure requirements. Amounts raised and contributed to each candidate must be reported to the FEC at specified intervals. Such reports are available for public scrutiny. Contribution limits are set at $5,000 per candidate per election. If a corporation chooses to establish more than one committee, the limit of contributions from all such committees to any one candidate remains $5,000.[2]

Through the legislation of the 1970s, Congress has given a new legal recognition and status to corporate PACs and provided a more precise definition of the scope and limits of their activities. It is fair to say,

1

however, that full public legitimacy, as distinguished from legality, thus far has not been achieved by corporate PACs. Much of the electorate is only dimly aware of the growth of PACs and how they work, but large segments of it view the role of money in politics with suspicion. It is relatively easy for organized giving through corporate PACs to be perceived by the public as creating too much indebtedness on the part of favored candidates to business and its interests. Corporate PACs on the whole have not had a good image with the press. The little attention that media have given them has been pervaded by the theme that money buys influence, that it demands and receives a return in favors and even votes. Sectors of opinion in the country that have perennially harbored fears about the degree of corporate impact on the political process have been quick to see in PACs a new engine for the exercise of undue political weight by business. Interest groups that have suffered legislative rebuffs and defeats in Congress in recent years have attributed their frustration, at least in part, to business-PAC giving. Worried observers have urged that corporate PACs have the potential to become so numerous and to raise and spend so much money that their concentrated power could overwhelm the political process. A great amount of cynicism continues to be expressed in these quarters about how truly voluntary the monetary support given by management-level employees to their PACs really is. Fund raising in the context of an employer-employee relationship is alleged to be inherently coercive. The separation between the corporation and its PAC is viewed as a fiction, and the corporation's top managment is assumed to dominate the PAC and to decide how its money will be spent with little room for participation or exertion of influence by the PAC's contributor constituency.

In Congress itself, two efforts, each of which proved abortive, were made either to roll back the spending capabilities of PACs in House races (the Obey-Railsback bill) or to render candidates less dependent on special-interest contributions by adoption of public funding (H.R. 1).[3] Major elements in the Democratic party (and at least a few Republicans) began to show signs of growing uncertainty about the potential impact of PACs on the voting habits and independence of congressmen and upon the political balance in Congress. The new Republican ascendancy in the Senate and major Republican gains in the House in November 1980 rendered it unlikely that changes in election-campaign legislation that might adversely affect corporate PACs would be high on the agenda of that Congress. But the legitimacy of corporate PACs as a vehicle of business expression in politics is likely to continue, for the foreseeable future, to be a vexing matter of controversy both in Congress and with the public at large.

This book aims at making a contribution to public enlightenment about corporate PACs and their activities by focusing on the fund-raising and fund-disbursing behavior and the internal organizational life of a sample of

PACs active in the congressional elections of 1978 and 1980. More generally, the intention is to enlarge the stock of empirical knowledge about the nature of business activity in politics. Some of the findings, for example, have a bearing on such major issues of concern to students of interest-group politics as the motivations that prompt managers to exert political influence, and the nature and extent of the limits to such influence. Evidence is developed relating to the question of the degree of internal political cohesion to be found in the business community. No public-policy recommendations are ventured, but this does not mean that the findings do not have implications for policy. In the minds of the authors, the findings do not appear to support some of the more dire fears and expectations that have been expressed about the probable consequences of the continued activities of corporate PACs. Although they cannot be said to constitute disproof, the findings point to developments and tendencies that are not readily compatible with the worst-case possibilities projected by corporate-PAC critics.

The book begins with an analysis of the expenditure patterns of the PACs in the sample in the elections of 1978 and 1980. Contrary to what seemed an emerging consensus that corporate PACs pursue a strategy of maximizing access to incumbents, a principal finding of the research is that, in the election of 1978, a group of PACs broke sharply from the preoccupation with access and focused a significant part of their money on assistance to challengers. In result, diversity in corporate PAC giving emerged, and such diversity was found to be at work again in the election of 1980. Two broad streams of PAC expenditure were in evidence, a predominantly pragmatic trend in which major emphasis was placed on cultivating access to incumbents, and a second, more ideological trend in which the preoccupation was in helping to bring about change in the political composition of the Congress. The variation in patterns of corporate-PAC giving inevitably raises the question of what factors constitute the basis for such variation, and a number of possible explanations are examined. Differences in the nature of the regulatory environments with which corporations interface are found to have a central influence on the adoption of corporate-PAC-contribution strategies. It is argued that variation in corporate-PAC-contribution strategies reflects an internal pluralism to be found within the corporate community that, in turn, limits the exertion of corporate-political influence.

The third chapter is concerned with PAC fund-raising activities. The various policies PACs have adopted in this area are examined. The principal finding is that corporate PACs have been generally reluctant, for a variety of reasons, to do all that the law permits, and that, in the main, they have avoided fund-raising policies that risk offending solicitees and that raise issues of legality. A kind of phenomenon of imperfect mobilization was discerned operating in the area of fund raising. This finding does not lend support to the expectations of some observers that corporate-PAC growth is destined to be exponential and to result in inordinate business influence on the political process. To the contrary, the research findings suggest that there are serious and inherent limits on the amounts of money that individual PACs can raise, and that aggregate corporate-PAC growth is not likely to be exponential. (Similarly, in chapter 4 it is argued that there are a number of factors persuading a significant number of large enterprises to refrain from chartering PACs.)

Chapter 4 deals principally with the governance of PACs. It examines the composition of the committees and their decision-making processes. It explores the extent of participation and influence of chief-executive officers (CEOs) and contributor constituencies in PAC affairs. A main finding is that PACs, as organizations, embody a mixture of hierarchical elements blended, however uneasily, with elements of voluntarism, representativeness, and accountability.

The work concludes with a review of PAC-officer evaluations of the PAC experience and their anticipations about future developments. It is hypothesized that the two streams of corporate-PAC giving that were earlier discerned are related to important differences in political perceptions and attitudes, and, ultimately, in political outlook that exist within the business community.

Sample and Data Base

The observations and generalizations made in this study of the behavior of corporate PACs, it should be understood, are focused particularly on those PACs that are associated with large corporations. The study sample consisted of seventy-one PACs affiliated with major American corporations. Over 85 percent of the PACs in the study are found in *Fortune*-listed companies. Of the *Fortune* list of the 500 leading industrial corporations, 202 had PACs active in the 1978 election; forty-six of these, or 23 percent, are represented in the sample. Of five *Fortune* lists (fifty each) of a total of 250 leading nonindustrials, 119 had PACs active in 1978; of these twenty, or 17 percent, are represented in the sample.[4] Banks, utilities, diversified financials, transportation, and retailing companies were included among the nonindustrials. A wide spectrum of industrials was included: oil-and-gas production, motor vehicles, metals and metal products, office equipment, food, chemicals and pharmaceuticals, electronics and appliances, steel, aerospace, rubber and plastics, paper products, publishing and printing. An effort was made also to achieve significant geographical representation. Companies in the sample have national headquarters located in major urban centers in the Northeast, Midwest, the Sunbelt, and the Far West.

Although the corporations studied were typically large scale, this is fully compatible with wide dispersion in size of PACs. Thirty-three of the seventy-one PACs in the sample were in the top-100 corporate PACs classified by amount of expenditures in the 1977-1978 congressional-election cycle. Six were in the top-twelve corporate PACs in the country by expenditures.[5] It should be noted that it was sufficient to spend slightly more than $40,000 for a corporate PAC to be included in the top 100. Almost 600 of the PACs active in the 1978 congressional election spent under $40,000 apiece. The great majority of corporate PACs are of modest size, including those affiliated with large corporations. It is not uncommon for billion-dollar corporations to have, in the phrase of one PAC officer, "paltry PACs."

The study data-base consisted of interviews with a key officer of each PAC, reviews of bylaws describing the formal criteria used by the PACs in making candidate-support decisions, PAC-contribution reports submitted to their members, and FEC computer printouts of the reports disclosing all contributions made to candidates in the 1978 and 1980 congressional-election cycles. In addition, interviews were conducted with staff members of the congressional committees concerned with the election-campaign laws, with staff of major business organizations concerned with encouragement of the emergence and growth of corporate PACs (Chamber of Commerce, National Association of Manufacturers, Public Affairs Council), with officers of nonconnected ideological PACs, and with representatives of interest groups and organizations with important perspectives to contribute on the corporate-PAC phenomenon (AFL-CIO, Common Cause, Congress Watch).

2 Campaign-Contribution Strategies: A Microanalysis

Perceptions of PAC Strategies

Thus far, corporate PACs have been active, to a major degree, in four complete congressional-election cycles. This relatively short life, however, has not prevented the emergence of strong impressions, generated by a variety of observers with very different commitments to and attitudes toward the PAC phenomenon, about the dominant trend of PAC giving. Perceptions of PAC-contribution policies have been heavily dependent on data supplied at intervals by the FEC. Two characteristics of FEC disclosure to the media—a primary focus on macrostatistics and a chronic time-lag in reporting what PACs are currently doing—have played a part in furthering widely prevalent, oversimplified (if not mistaken), impressions of what corporate PACs have been doing with their money. Emphasis on reporting total amounts donated to all candidates and total amounts contributed to parties, incumbents, challengers, and open-seat contestants have tended to foster the view that PAC giving is unidirectional and that there is a single modal type of corporate PAC. Such aggregate figures, valuable as they are, have obscured the extent of diversity among individual corporate PACs in their patterns of giving. The most significant development in PAC giving in the 1977-1978 election cycle was the emergence of a set of corporate PACs that have defined a new identity for themselves and broken sharply from the incumbency-access orientation that the aggregate statistics seemed to show was the continuing dominant tendency in PAC giving.

At the very time that observers were explaining that corporate PACs were defensive and passive givers, a sizable number were adopting an aggressive posture in support of challengers to incumbents. Not until the winter of 1979 did FEC reporting catch up with what corporate PACs had, in fact, been doing. In February 1979, FEC data showed that corporate PACs had reserved a large part of their funds for contributions in the last weeks of the campaign and that these funds had been channeled heavily to Republicans and challengers. Final data in May 1979 showed that corporate PACs in the aggregate had favored Republican challengers by almost two to one and that the percentage of totals spent on challengers had increased considerably in comparison to the 1976 election. But as late as November 1978, the FEC was reporting that corporate PACs were still giving heavily to incumbents and that Republicans were receiving only slightly more than half of their contributions.[1]

Because of the lag in FEC reporting and the even longer delay in assimilating the meaning of the latest figures, a large volume of the commentary on corporate PACs in 1978 and well into 1979 was based upon some assumptions about their behavior in the election of 1978 that turned out to be contrary to fact. A responsible business source, for example, in the summer of 1979 summarized the history of corporate PAC spending as follows:

> At the close of the first year in which substantial corporate PAC money was made available to candidates and parties (1976) . . . as much money was contributed to Democrats as Republicans. In 1977, more money went to Democrats than to Republicans, and the earliest figures in 1978 indicated that the trend was continuing.[2]

The Conference Board's analysis of PAC-contribution policy was entirely devoted to explaining why so much was given to Democrats and incumbents.

Prominent Republican politicians expressed discomfort with the trend of corporate-PAC giving in 1977 and the early months of 1978. They were frankly disappointed that corporate PACs were showing an apparent inclination to give so heavily to incumbents of the other party. Representative Vanderjagt, chairman of the House GOP Campaign Committee, noted tartly that the public perceives Republicans as "carrying business' water," but "much of big business is supporting our enemy."[3] The Republican National Committee was reputed to be considering the issue of a "dirty list" of corporate PACs that, despite conservative rhetoric, gave largely to Democrats. And a quip by Ronald Reagan in a speech to corporate government-relations officers came to be widely quoted: "The best thing you can hope for by following an anti-business incumbent contribution policy is that the alligator will eat you last."[4]

There is evidence that during 1978 a vigorous discussion among corporate PACs was taking place about their contribution trends. Letters written by Donald M. Kendall and Justin Dart, top corporate executives active in politics and in their own PACs, achieved wide circulation. Both expressed shock that so much corporate-PAC giving seemed to be so little attentive to candidates' records "on the broader, free enterprise issues." Kendall called for a more "bifocal" approach in PAC giving, with an appropriate mix of support for both incumbents and challengers; Dart more militantly urged the adoption of a clear-cut strategy of seeking to alter the political composition of Congress.[5] However, some friends of corporate PACs, in their defense, observed that PACs were showing an ability to pick and choose among Democrats. Not all Democratic incumbents receiving PAC funds were antibusiness. By one such observer's count, at least fifty House Democrats were as probusiness as any of the Republicans.[6]

The criticisms and admonitions emanating from Republicans and corporate leaders appear to have had important effects on PAC thinking during 1978. The discussion provided an additional impetus to those PACs that were already moving in a new direction toward support of challengers. This helps to account for the late surge of money for Republicans and challengers reflected in the 1979 press releases of the FEC. The corporate PACs that were determined, in the face of criticism, to continue along the path of support for incumbents were obliged to develop defensible rationales for their behavior. PACs, in whatever direction they proceeded, were stimulated to engage in a more self-conscious examination of the implications of what they were doing.

While movement toward a greater complexity in styles of corporate-PAC giving was in fact underway, there appeared a profusion of anlayses that sought to account for an assumed uniform fixation on incumbents. Representatives of major-interest groups suffering serious defeats of legislative proposals in Congress attributed their reverses to the growing impact of increased corporate-PAC giving. In their view, the support of incumbents concerned buying influence. The most widely repeated cynical observation about corporate-PAC support of so many Democratic incumbents was to the effect that PACs owned one party and were proceeding to buy another. Incumbency orientation was seen as providing more evidence of the amoral nature of corporate executives. Even though they had no love of the Democrats, they supported them on practical grounds. Short-run interests took precedence over ideological preferences. Holders of this view predicted confidently that corporate PACs would not support Republicans overwhelmingly until Republicans had become the majority party in Congress.[7]

Officers of nonconnected PACs of a New Right persuasion were scornful of corporate PAC spending policies. One attributed them to dominance of the committees by rank political amateurs who had no "strategic concept" of what they wanted to accomplish with their money. They were unable to grasp the value of a consistent policy of favoring their ideological friends and opposing their ideological enemies. On the other hand, corporate leaders who were dissatisfied with PAC spending trends were more likely to attribute them to the influence of professionals on the committees, particularly the Washington representatives.[8]

Academic students of campaign finance produced their own analysis of corporate PAC addiction to incumbents. They suggested that corporations placed a premium on avoiding controversy and saw campaign contributions as an activity peripheral to the main business of the firm. PAC giving was passive; that is, it was a response to requests initiated by candidates. For defensive reasons PACs wanted to be on the side of winners, and the safe response, therefore, was to favor incumbents, regardless of ideological differences. The point to be urged about such interpretations is not that they were wrong, but that they assumed that PAC behavior was uniform at a time when it was growing more diverse and complex. Such explanations addressed only one of the trends in PAC contribution strategy, even as two mainstreams of PAC giving were making their appearance in the 1978 election.[9]

In 1979 two legislative efforts were made to curb what was seen as the threat of the growth of excessive PAC influence. The first, calling for partial public financing of House campaigns, failed to be reported out of the Committee on House Administration. The second, the Obey-Railsback bill, passed the House in October 1979. It provided for reduced limits in House races on the amounts that individual PACs could contribute to each candidate, and also placed a new limit on the amounts that all PACs might contribute to any candidate. Opponents charged that incumbency protection was the main preoccupation of the Democratic House leadership in bringing the bill to the floor. In reply, supporters pointed to figures showing that incumbents received the bulk of funds expended by all kinds of PACs. Curbing PAC expenditures, therefore, would have its largest impact on incumbents. Opponents then explained their position more explicitly: In 1978 corporate PACs had shown signs of shifting much more money to challengers. The Democratic leadership was responding, therefore, to the new prospect that the larger part of corporate PAC funds in the future might be placed at the disposal of Republican challengers.[10]

In this debate there is an explicit recognition of the complexity of corporate-PAC giving, an awareness that it is not single directional and cannot be summed up as access-incumbency oriented. It would substitute one exaggeration for another, however, to see PACs as uniformly dropping the previous strategy and adopting instead an aggressive challenger-oriented stance. What the evidence points to is that challenger-oriented corporate PACs made their appearance to a significant degree in the 1978 election, that this tendency in PAC giving continued in 1980, but that the earlier incumbency-access orientation persists as well.

The most recent academic studies have acknowledged the diversity in PAC strategies. The Kennedy School of Government report on campaign finance commissioned by the Committee on House Administration, although committed still to the notion of the defensive and passive nature of corporate-PAC giving, also took note that the 1978 FEC data showed that they "learned faster than . . . anticipated."[11] The clearest recognition of corporate-PAC differentiation appears in the work of Michael Malbin who distinguishes between what he calls special-interest and general-interest PACs.[12]

PAC Diversity: Six Vignettes

Interview data provide important clues to the existence of PAC differentiation in patterns of giving, as the following summaries of descriptions of their contribution strategies by officers of six representative PACs illustrate.

1. In 1978 PAC I decided to take up a vanguard position among corporate PACs and to place much less emphasis on support of incumbents. It assisted over eighty candidates in 1978, two-thirds of whom were challengers and open-seat contestants. PAC I's overriding commitment is to work for major change in the philosophical attitudes of the Congress. The parent corporation understands that, in a complex society, some regulation is necessary, but the conviction runs deep among its executives and shareholders that overregulation has become a severe problem. Changing the political complexion of Congress is seen as centrally related to the task of creating a more constructive and helpful regulatory environment for business. PAC I views itself as bipartisan, even though over 90 percent of its money goes to Republicans. It would like to support Democrats who share its political views, but, outside of the South, they are hard to find. PAC I does not want to be identified as a Republican PAC and hopes that the rising conservative mood in the country will make it possible to support more Democrats. It emphasizes that it does not seek to buy influence with its money. It makes no conditional offers of its funds and aims at no special consideration for its support.

2. PAC II does not judge congressmen on the basis of their positions on single issues, even though some of these might be important to the parent corporation. Candidates, instead, are evaluated on the basis of their general economic views, with special emphasis on their attitudes toward government regulation and fiscal responsibility. The PAC tries to help defeat incumbents that are indifferent or hostile to the political and economic values of the corporation's executives. It supports challengers and open-seat contestants even more heavily than does PAC I. Fifty percent of total money spent went to candidates who lost their races in 1978. But the PAC officer has no regrets. His main interest is in working for change, not in compiling a good won-lost record. PAC II is not seeking "smiling access." Significant amounts are contributed to primaries and to challengers early in their campaigns. With few exceptions, the Democrats it supports have highly conservative voting records.

3. PAC III defines its central purpose as helping to bring about a "better balanced Congress." It gives more heavily to incumbent Democrats than does PAC I or PAC II. The PAC officer observes, however, that the key question for him is not whether business PACs give to Democrats, but rather, to which Democrats they give. Both parties, in his view, contain members who want less inflation, expansion of exports, and a more favorable climate

for capital formation and business growth. The Democrats supported by PAC III generally rank as high in probusiness and conservative voting ratings as Republicans. The PAC works on the basis of a 50 percent rule in assessing incumbents. It will not ordinarily give money to those they rate above 50 percent in liberal-labor ratings. However, the requirements of a constituency relationship led in three instances in 1978 to the waiving of the 50 percent rule. Because there is an important company site in the districts with a large number of employees, and because PAC members know and value the incumbents, PAC III contributed to candidates who might otherwise have been on its list of rejections. PAC III reserves at least one-third of its funds for challengers and open-seat contestants; it tries to find races where its help could make a difference. The PAC officer condemns the practice of giving money to incumbents because of committee assignments. In his view this is not a good reason to contribute to a candidate with an otherwise unacceptable voting record.

4. PAC IV's spokesman explains that donations are made primarily to incumbents in districts where the company has facilities and there is a constituency relationship. Whether the candidate favors free enterprise is considered, but so far minimal amounts have been devoted to challengers. A key factor here is the hand-to-mouth amounts raised by the PAC. The essential question about an incumbent is whether he has "done us some service, not is he 100 percent O.K." The corporation has a substantial constituency relationship with one-fourth of the House and two-thirds of the Senate. The PAC's contribution policies are well settled and not likely to alter much. It will continue to contribute to incumbents whom its Washington representatives lobby on pertinent issues four or five times a year and who have proven responsive. The PAC has given to more Democrats than Republicans, but more of its total money has gone to Republicans (higher average contributions). The PAC spokesman acknowledges the criticisms of those who think that PACs should concentrate on trying to get "new blood, new thinking" into the Congress. But incumbency, he stresses, especially in the House, is a fact to be lived with, and there is much that he considers right in the current makeup of Congress.

5. PAC V's officer, a Washington lobbyist, is unmoved by the annoyance expressed in some circles with PACs that give undue support to incumbent Democrats: "We do what is best for us." Corporations do not all have the same interests. There is no single business view of what is wanted in Washington. On some matters business views may even collide. The corporation's top managers are custodians of the shareholders' investment and want to obtain results on company-related issues. There is an immediate interest, for example, in tariffs. Incumbent Democratic liberals can be brought to see the importance of being supportive on an issue such as protection that affects employment and wages in their districts.

PAC V's approach is one of accommodation and "working within the political process;" it is not after transformation. The PAC officer admits that some executives choose not to contribute to the PAC because they are offended by its support of too many Democrats. He replies that PAC donations have nothing to do with party. The PAC has an "interest orientation." The corporation operates in twenty states, and, in particular, in some twenty districts in these states. A donation is always given to the incumbents in these districts. A few committees have jurisdiction over subject matter with special significance for the company's welfare. The PAC cannot afford to give to all members of such committees. Instead it gives to the members who are especially influential in committee decision making. The PAC will not support challengers to incumbents on committees that the Washington lobbyist has reason to believe would be helpful on a company-related issue.

The modest amounts that are given to incumbents cannot "lock up a member." But it is important for incumbents who participate in decisions that affect the corporation to know that "we have some interest in keeping them in office." Great numbers of people compete for the attention of congressmen. It helps to get into a member's office, if one is known to have given him some help. "But then you have to persuade him. The donation won't do this for you." PAC V's contributions involve "opening doors" and "keeping them from being closed." The PAC officer attaches importance to "being with the winner." If the PAC backs a loser, it contributes to defray the deficit of the successful challenger.

6. PAC VI's manager states that "our top consideration is the races in our geographical territory." The corporation (a railroad) operates in fifteen states. Also, donations are made outside these states to members of the House transportation subcommittee. The subcommittee chairman is supported, because "he thinks with us on certain legislation." Money was not given to his opponent, a philosophical conservative, who observed bitterly that some PACs give only to incumbents, even those who advocate extending the power and influence of the federal government. The PAC purchases many tickets to fund raisers in order "to maintain contacts." It gives to more Democrats than Republicans, "because there are so many of them." Party affiliation is not significant; it is committee membership and constituency relationship that count. The company operates in a heavily regulated environment where what happens on Capitol Hill directly "affects the bottom line."

These vignettes are representative of the diversity of attitudes among PACs on what is appropriate use of their money. There are differences among PACs in conception of purpose, ranging from those who seek to alter the political balance to those who have a pure interest, almost an apolitical orientation. Some are focused almost exclusively on constituency service from incumbents; others attach minimal significance to such service. Some attach key importance to membership on relevant committees; others believe such membership is not by itself valid reason for donating money. Some give heavily, indeed almost exclusively, to Republicans and want the GOP to become the majority party. Others give to both parties, but again with differences in emphasis. Some will give only to conservatives in both parties; others give to liberal-labor-oriented Democrats, out of interest considerations. Some are contemptuous of "smiling access;" for others "keeping doors open" is what it is all about. For some the criticism of PACs for fixation on incumbents plainly has been taken to heart; others give every sign that they do not intend to be deflected from a chosen course by such criticism.

Two Mainstreams of PAC Giving

Corporate PACs are not behaving in a uniform way, nor are they pursuing similar goals and seeking identical results. To the contrary, the position taken in this study is that there are two major directions in PAC giving. In broad terms, corporate PACs tend to be either predominantly ideological or pragmatic in orientation. PACs differ, first, in the degree to which they are motivated by the goal of helping to bring about significant political change. The ideological PAC is seeking to alter the political composition of Congress, to help produce a conservative or Republican majority in both houses or, failing that, to induce a movement in a more conservative and pro-business direction—in any case to move the center of gravity of the Congress to the Right. For the pragmatic PAC, the priority is to accommodate, in what it regards as a realistic way, the existing composition of Congress, and to secure and maintain a high degree of access to incumbent elected officials, with some, but not heavy, emphasis on party affiliation.

Corporate PACs differ, furthermore, in the breadth or narrowness of the scope of issues on which they base their judgments concerning the appropriateness of giving or withholding support to candidates. For the ideological PAC the stance of a candidate on a range of general business issues is paramount, because this stance indicates whether the candidate understands and is responsive to the requirements for effective functioning of the business system. The ideological PAC acts on the belief that the needs and interests of the parent corporation are best served by contributing to the support of candidates that show some overall commitment to the enterprise and to the market as an alternative to regulation. For the pragmatic PAC, the key consideration is whether the candidate can be expected to be accessible and supportive of the corporation on some special issues or issues that impact directly and immediately on the well-being or the viability of the firm. For such PACs, it is permissible to make donations to candidates on this ground, even if they show signs of indifference or hostility on broader issues relating to the business system. The pragmatic PAC may invoke the symbolism of free enterprise in its literature, but its concrete decisions will be made on the basis of the candidate's perceived responsiveness to specific interests of the corporation, without much regard to stance on free enterprise.

In summary, the ideogical PAC typically is change oriented, secondarily interested in access, and judges candidates primarily on the basis of stands on a spectrum of issues that indicate degree of sympathy for the enterprise system. The pragmatic PAC adapts to the existing balance of political forces, seeks primarily to enhance access, and judges candidates on their stance on specific company-related issues.

A Typology of PACs

An effort was made to give more precise definition to this differentiation of corporate PACs by utilizing a number of quantitative indicators drawn from FEC data for the election of 1978 to identify the pragmatic or ideological orientation of the PACs in the sample, and, in effect, to construct a typology of PACs. The steps in the method adopted are set forth in summary form as follows:

1. Seven ratios were calculated for each PAC. These consisted of three incumbency ratios: (a) the total spent on House incumbents as a percentage of the total spent on all House candidates, (b) the total spent on Senate incumbents as a percentage of the total spent on all Senate incumbents, and (c) the total spent on all House-Senate incumbents as a percentage of the total spent on all House-Senate candidates. Three Republican-party-support ratios were also calculated: (a) the total spent on Republican candidates in the House as a percentage of the total spent on all House candidates, (b) the total spent on Republican candidates in the Senate as a percentage of the total spent on all Senate candidates, and (c) the total spent on Republican candidates in House and Senate as a percentage of the total spent on all House-Senate candidates. Finally, the total spent on House liberal Democrats was figured. A liberal Democrat was defined as a Democratic incumbent who received a rating of 70 percent or above from either the Americans for Democratic Action (ADA) or AFL-CIO Committee on Political

Education (COPE).[13] These ratios serve as important indicators of the pragmatic or ideological orientation of PACs. The incumbency and party-support ratios offer clues to whether a PAC is focused on change in the party composition of Congress or on improving access. Low incumbency ratios combined with high Republican-party-support ratios indicate an ideological PAC, just as high incumbency-ratios and low Republican-party-support ratios indicate an ideological PAC, just as high incumbency-ratios and low Republican-party-support ratios indicate a pragmatic PAC. The liberal Democrat ratio is a significant indicator of whether a PAC judges candidates in terms of industry-specific issues or more general attitudes towards the business system.

2. To decide whether PACs showed high or low incumbency or Republican-party-support ratios required reference points that were drawn from FEC statistics of PAC giving in the election of 1978. The data show that the incumbency ratio for all corporate PAC giving was 59 percent and that the Republican-party-support ratio was 63 percent. PACs that had incumbency ratios below 59 percent and Republican-support-ratios above 63 percent were identified as ideological, and PACs in reverse positions were considered pragmatic. A PAC was considered to have a high liberal-Democrat-support ratio if more than 30 percent of its total contributions to incumbent House Democrats went to liberals.

3. The PACs in the sample were distributed along a continuum, as appears in table 2-1.

An index number (1.0-4.0) was assigned to each of the seven ratios per PAC according to where the ratio fit in the diagram (I-IV). Adding the seven scores and dividing by seven gave a numerical average that permitted the assignment of each PAC to a position on the continuum. Four modal

Table 2-1
Typology of PACS
(percentage)

	Type I Ideological (1.0-1.5)	Type II Ideological Leaning (1.6-2.5)	Type III Pragmatic Leaning (2.8-3-4)	Type IV Pragmatic (3.5-4.0)
Incumbency Ratios	0-50	51-59	60-79	80-100
Republican-Party- Support Ratios	100-80	79-63	62-51	50-0
Liberal-Democrat/ Incumbent House- Democrat Ratios	0-20	21-30	31-40	41 +

patterns could be identified: I. Ideological, pure type; II. Ideological leaning, hybrid type; III. Pragmatic leaning, hybrid type; IV. Pragmatic, pure
type. Types I and IV were designated as pure types because of the high
degree of internal consistency among the seven ratios, producing for the
Type I PACs numerical averages between 1.0-1.5, and the Type IV PACs
averages between 3.5-4.0. Thirty-eight percent of the sample in 1978 was in
Type I or Type IV. Thus the majority of the PACs did not exhibit the high
degree of consistency among the seven ratios found in Types I and IV and
were classified as hybrid types. On balance, each of these PACs inclined
either more to the ideological side (averages from 1.6-2.5) or to the
pragmatic side (averages from 2.8-3.4) of the continuum, and were, therefore, designated as ideological leaning (Type II), or pragmatic leaning (Type
III). (Eight percent of the PACs in the sample, in the middle of the continuum [2.6-2.7], were classified as indeterminate.)

The characteristic features of each PAC type may be summarized as
follows.

Type I (ideological): These PACs show an unequivocal commitment to
the goal of change in party composition and in the philosophical attitudes
of Congress. At least 50 percent of their contributions were channeled to
challengers and open-seat candidates; at least 80 percent of these went to
Republicans. Incumbent Democrats correspondingly received only a small
part of their money and liberal Democrats obtained under 15 percent of the
amounts given to such incumbents.

Type II (ideological leaning): These PACs show a more bifocal approach than the Type I PACs, but with clearly discernible emphasis on
ideological considerations. They gave a higher percentage of contributions
to incumbents. Nevertheless, at least a third or more of their money was
devoted to support of challengers and open-seat contestants. They do not
exclude the desirability of change in the party composition of Congress but
seem more concerned with helping to produce a Congress that, even if remaining in control of Democrats, will be on terms more favorable to
business. Their Republican-support ratios were significantly higher than the
all-PAC average (63 percent) but lower than those of the Type I PACs.
Although they gave more heavily to Democrats than did Type I PACs, a
real effort was made to limit such giving to Democrats who were conservative and probusiness. For example, two-thirds of the group gave under a
third of the money going to incumbent Democrats to liberals. These PACs
are likely to feel apologetic when they give to a liberal, and when asked
about it, show a need to justify it at some length.

Type III (pragmatic leaning): These PACs, although more bifocal in
approach than Type IV PACs, show a definite tilt in a pragmatic direction.
Seventy-five percent of them had incumbency ratios in 1978 that were
higher than the all-PAC average (59 percent). Their Republican-support

ratios ran below the all-PAC average (63 percent). However, over half of them, unlike Type IV PACs, gave somewhat more of their money to Republicans than Democrats. They contributed, without discomfort, to substantial numbers of House liberal Democrats among incumbents.

Type IV (pragmatic): These PACs display an exclusive focus on winning access to incumbents. Three-fourths of the PACs in this group spent 85 percent or more of their money on incumbents. They engaged in little risk taking on behalf of challengers. Three-fourths of the group gave over 50 percent of their money to Democrats. Also, half of them gave liberals over 50 percent of the sums they contributed to incumbent House Democrats.

The method of analysis here points to a considerable dispersion of PAC strategies, confirms the existence of the two broad streams in PAC strategies previously postulated, and indicates, furthermore, that an additional element of PAC diversity appears in the varying degrees of single-mindedness with which PACs follow ideological or pragmatic trends in their giving.

Corporate-PAC Impact on the Electoral
Overturn of 1980

Nonconnected PACs that are ideologically conservative have lately achieved notoriety because of their seemingly highly successful utilization of independent expenditures permitted under the law to wage advertising campaigns to unseat incumbent liberal Democrats. The resounding defeat, in 1980, of a whole set of such liberal notables in the Senate has prompted some to make claims and others to raise alarms about the effectiveness or legitimacy of the independent strategies pursued by the nonconnected PACs. Logicians might be tempted instead to warn against the dangers of *post hoc ergo propter hoc.*

Although great care must be used in attempting to relate PAC-contribution strategy to election outcomes, it is contended here that the analysis pursued in this study permits at least tentative inferences concerning the probable impact of corporate-PAC money on the electoral results of 1980. Such inferences will be drawn on the basis of (1) a comparison of the patterns of giving of the PACs in the sample in 1978 and 1980, and (2) an analysis of the aggregate expenditures of the PACs in the sample in the pivotal races in which Democratic seats were captured by Republicans.

1. Corporate-PAC strategies in 1978 and 1980: Table 2-2 shows the distribution of the seventy-one PACs in the sample by contribution strategy in 1978 and 1980.

Of the nineteen PACs classified as Type I in 1978, none made a fundamental shift in strategy in 1980. (By fundamental is meant a change in

Table 2-2
Corporate-PAC Strategies in 1978 and 1980

	Type I (Ideological)	Type II (Ideological Leaning)	Type III (Pragmatic Leaning)	Type IV (Pragmatic)	(Indeterminate)
1978	19	21	17	8	6
1980	15	23	8	20	5

broad classification from ideological (I-II) to pragmatic (III-IV), or vice versa, or from either broad classification to indeterminate.) Six of the nineteen, however, moved from Type I to Type II, a minor shift reflecting higher incumbency ratios that were the result of increased support for conservative incumbents of both parties.

Of the twenty-one PACs classified as Type II in 1978, seven made a fundamental shift in 1980 to pragmatic (III-IV) or indeterminate. Two of the twenty-one made a minor shift to Type I.

Of the seventeen PACs classified as Type III in 1978, two made a fundamental shift (one each to ideological leaning and indeterminate). Twelve made a minor shift to Type IV.

Of the eight PACs classified as Type IV in 1978, two made a fundamental shift (one each to ideological leaning and indeterminate).

The six PACs classified as indeterminate in 1978 were reclassified as either ideological (3) or pragmatic (3) in 1980.

Comparison of the arrays for 1978 and 1980 reveals the relative stability of the patterns of PAC giving that emerged in 1978. Eighty-three percent of the PACs in the sample classified as ideological (I-II) or pragmatic (III-IV) remained within the same broad classifications in 1980. Only eleven such PACs made a fundamental shift of classification in 1980.

The major outcomes of the congressional election of 1980 were the emergence of a Republican majority in the Senate and the reestablishment of the basis for the dominance of a Republican-conservative-Democratic coalition in the House. If one were tempted to make inferences about probable corporate-PAC behavior from the electoral results of 1980, a further sharp turn in an ideological direction by many more PACs might have been anticipated. In fact, this development did not take place. Both streams of giving that had applied in 1978 continued in 1980, with a modest number of fundamental shifts in contribution strategies in 1980. Only four of the PACs previously identified as pragmatic or pragmatic leaning moved in a more ideological direction, two to indeterminate and two to ideological leaning. Moreover, the dominant tendency among PACs identified as pragmatic leaning in 1978 was to become more emphatically so in 1980. (Twelve of seventeen classified as pragmatic leaning—III could be identified as pragmatic—IV in 1980.) Also among those PACs identified as ideological leaning in 1978, one-third (seven) became less ideological in their strategies in 1980. Among the eleven PACs making a fundamental shift in 1980, seven became less ideological and four more so.

If one uses shifts of strategy by numbers of PACs as the indicator, the data suggest that the PACs in the sample tended, on balance, in a more pragmatic direction in 1980. In an election in which Republican challengers were outstandingly successful in both houses, it is startling to find that the corporate PACs in the sample seemed to move, if anything, slightly away from ideological giving—a trend not in concert with the major outcomes of the election.

2. Corporate PAC contributions in pivotal races (1978 and 1980): In the 1978 congressional elections, Republicans captured eight Democratic seats while losing five of their own, for a net gain of three. Two years later, Republicans took control of the Senate by virtue of their sweep of twelve Democratic seats without a single loss. Table 2-3 illustrates the divergent flow of the ideological (I-II) and pragmatic (III-IV) PACs' contributions in the eight Senate races in 1978 and the twelve in 1980 in which Democratic seats were lost to Republicans.

Ideological PACs (I-II) outspent their fellows by a two-to-one margin in all Senate races in each election, and, true to their professed goal to help bring about a more probusiness Congress, they dominated the funding of those Republican candidates who won Democratic seats, furnishing them with 84 percent of the sample PAC dollars received in 1978 and 90 percent in 1980. From another perspective, Types I and II PACs concentrated 33 percent of their total spending in 1978 ($225,233 out of $684,858) on the eight Republican nonincumbents who wrested Senate seats from Democrats and 40 percent ($390,040 out of $987,659) on the twelve Republicans who accomplished this feat in 1980.

At the same time these PACs, which comprised over half the sample, accounted for less than one-third of the total spent on the Democrats who lost Senate seats; and the sums they spent on the defeated Democrats in the two elections ($6,810 and $27,131, respectively) amounted to less than 1 percent of their total expenditures on Senate candidates. This contrasts significantly with the 33 percent and 40 percent portions targeted to the victorious Republicans, a contrast that brings into sharper focus the degree of importance these PACs attach to changing the status quo in Congress. It is notable, also, that the thrust of their spending in Senate campaigns accords with the shift in favor of Republican candidates voters manifested in both elections.

Types III and IV PACs, on the other hand, evinced little interest in abetting the Republican drive to seize control of the Senate, although in

Table 2-3
Contributions to Key Senate Races, by PAC Type, 1978 and 1980

PAC Type	Type I	Type II	Indeterminate	Type III	Type IV	Totals
1978						
Percentage of sample	26.8	29.6	8.4	23.9	11.3	100
Total contributions	$377,435	$307,423	$65,393	$188,074	$61,655	$ 999,980
Percentage of total	37.8	30.7	6.5	18.8	6.2	100
Total contributions to 8 Republican candidates	$154,000	$ 71,233	$20,600	$ 21,500	$ 1,500	$ 268,833
Percentage of Republican total	57.3	26.5	7.7	8.0	6.5	100
Total contributions to 8 Democratic candidates	$ 2,410	$ 4,400	$ 2,450	$ 7,350	$ 5,900	$ 22,510
Percentage of Democratic total	10.7	19.5	10.9	32.7	26.2	100
1980						
Percentage of sample	21.1	32.4	7.0	11.3	28.2	100
Total contributions	$495,198	$492,461	$53,730	$146,730	$305,459	$1,493,578
Percentage of total	33.2	33.0	3.6	9.8	20.4	100
Total contributions to 12 Republican candidates	$221,900	$177,140	$11,000	$ 11,800	$ 19,100	$ 440,940
Percentage of Republican total	50.3	40.2	2.5	2.7	4.3	100
Total contributions to 12 Democratic candidates	$ 11,100	$ 16,031	$ 5,800	$ 8,050	$ 44,025	$ 85,006
Percentage of Democratic total	13.0	18.9	6.8	9.5	51.8	100

1978 they did spend more money on the eight Republican contestants than on their Democratic opponents. Collectively, they accounted for 25 percent of all sample PAC spending in Senate races in 1978 and 30 percent in 1980; yet only 9 percent of their dollars in 1978 and 7 percent in 1980 went to the Republican aspirants.

Pragmatic-PAC support for the Democratic candidates in these twenty critical Senate races was proportionately higher—three-fifths of the total in each election—than that accorded them by the rest of the sample. But an examination of their aggregate-spending figures reveals these PACs on the whole as little interested in mounting a rescue effort to save endangered Democratic seats. Even as ideological PACs were pouring disproportionate amounts of their available funds into the coffers of the Republican challengers in these key races, pragmatic PACs earmarked a meager $13,250 for the eight beleaguered Democrats or 5 percent of the $249,729 they spent on all Senate races in 1978, and $52,075 for the twelve Democratic losers in 1980, 11 percent of their $452,189 total expenditures.

Table 2-4 shows similar divergent patterns of giving in the twenty-two House races in 1978 and the thirty-seven in 1980 in which Republicans took Democratic seats.

Types I and II PACs spent nearly twice as much on House races than did Types III and IV, and they supplied over 90 percent of sample PAC dollars given to the nonincumbent Republican winners in both elections. Their contributions, to these Republican candidates, of 15 percent of their total spending in 1978 ($153,585 out of $1,001,184) and 18 percent in 1980 ($313,545 out of $1,712,012), though below those they recorded in support of nonincumbent Republican winners in Senate races, were impressive, nevertheless, when placed within the context of 435 House races.

Types III and IV PACs, whose total House contributions comprised around one-third of all sample PAC spending, gave much more money to the Democrats who lost House seats than to their Republican opponents, but they targeted only 4 percent of their House dollars ($21,025 out of $480,035) to the twenty-two unsuccessful Democrats in 1978 and 8 percent ($65,476 out of $820,845) to the thirty-seven who lost seats in 1980. Their failure to provide substantial support to threatened Democratic congressmen suggests that pragmatic PACs have little interest in protecting endangered incumbents. On the other hand, they did not opt to join with the majority of voters who supported the Republicans in these turnover elections. Rather, they stood apart from these partisan battles and continued, instead, to distribute the bulk of their funds among incumbents favored to win.

Ideological PACs in the sample in 1978 and 1980 reserved a significant part of their funds for races identified as key, where Republican challengers or open-seat candidates were judged to have a real opportunity to win

Table 2-4
Contributions to Key House Races, by PAC Type, 1978 and 1980

PAC Type	Type I	Type II	Indeterminate	Type III	Type IV	Totals
1978						
Percentage of sample	26.8	29.6	8.4	23.9	11.3	100
Total contributions	$540,623	$460,561	$100,175	$365,995	$114,040	$1,581,394
Percentage of total	34.2	29.1	6.3	23.2	7.2	100
Total contributions to 22 Republican candidates	$100,251	$ 53,335	$ 4,500	$ 8,100	$ 2,350	$ 344,225
Percentage of Republican total	59.5	31.6	2.7	4.8	1.4	100
Total contributions to 22 Democratic candidates	$ 1,650	$ 11,950	$ 2,050	$ 16,525	$ 4,500	$ 103,176
Percentage of Democratic total	4.5	32.6	5.6	45.0	12.3	100
1980						
Percentage of sample	21.1	32.4	7.0	11.3	28.2	100
Total contributions	$892,727	$819,285	$ 95,055	$260,152	$560,693	$2,627,912
Percentage of total	34.0	31.2	3.6	9.9	21.3	100
Total contributions to 37 Republican candidates	$200,271	$113,274	$ 8,320	$ 12,700	$ 9,660	$ 344,225
Percentage of Republican total	58.2	32.9	2.4	3.7	2.8	100
Total contributions to 37 Democratic candidates	$ 7,750	$ 27,200	$ 2,950	$ 14,350	$ 51,126	$ 103,176
Percentage of Democratic total	7.3	26.4	2.9	13.9	49.5	100

previously held and vulnerable Democratic seats. Although acting without visible coordination from any single external source, they found their way independently and, with considerable sophistication, to these pivotal races. The result, in the aggregate, was the concentration of high percentages of available dollars in support of the Republican candidates in these races. In 1980, in particular, their behavior was highly consonant with the electoral outcomes in the races concerned, although, of course, this by itself says little about how decisively their spending efforts contributed to bringing about the desired outcomes.

On the other hand, the pragmatic PACs in the sample expended a relatively minor share of their total funds on these pivotal races. They showed little of the inclination of the ideological PACs to assist the Republican candidates in them, although it is true that they gave higher percentages of their totals expended in these races to Republicans than the ideological PACs were willing to devote to Democrats. However, in 1980 the pragmatic PACs gave the majority of the funds devoted to these races to the incumbent Democrats with whom, presumably, they had established relationships.

Despite the concentrated effort of the ideological PACs on behalf of Republican contestants in the pivotal races in 1980, diversity in the patterns of corporate-PAC giving was still strongly present and was operating to produce some dilution of the corporate-PAC impact on the electoral overturn of 1980.

Explanation of Variation in PAC Strategies

In this section, five hypotheses intended to explain variation in PAC campaign contribution strategies are examined. Consideration is given to suggestions that the ideological or pragmatic orientation of PACs is significantly related to (1) the size of PACs, measured by contribution totals; (2) the role of the Washington representative in PAC decision making; (3) the degree of diversification in the economic activities of the parent corporation; (4) the industrial or nonindustrial character of the parent corporation; and (5) the nature of the regulatory environment that the parent corporation confronts, and its perception of and attitudes towards that environment.

1. The size of PACs measured by contribution totals: A careful observer of the PAC scene commenting recently on the activities of corporate PACs in preparation for the 1980 campaign relates the differences in patterns of PAC giving to the simple factor of size. The larger the PAC, he asserts, the more likely it is to become involved in congressional races outside the districts where the parent corporation maintains plants or other locations and to project itself into races that pit a probusiness candidate

against one who is not so identified. The larger PACs are more inclined, in his view, to be committed to a central purpose of contributing to the election of a more business-oriented Congress, and such purpose sets the direction of their campaign giving. The smaller corporate PACs have more "limited goals"; they do not feel able to try to "shape Congress" as the larger ones do.[14]

An effort was made to test the hypothesis that pragmatic and ideological patterns of giving are related in important degree to PAC size. The PACs in the sample were distributed in a continuum according to the amount of total contribution to congressional candidates in the 1978 and 1980 elections. Table 2-5 shows the results by quartiles and upper and lower halves of the distribution.

The results are roughly similar for both years. Three out of five Type I (ideological) and Type II (ideological leaning) PACs are found in the upper half of the distribution; on the other hand, three out of five Type III (pragmatic leaning) and Type IV (pragmatic) PACs are found in the lower half of the distribution. In addition, it should be noted that all the PACs in the sample that contributed $100,000 or more in the 1980 election were either Type I or Type II PACs. If one calculates the average total contribu-

Table 2-5
Size of PAC and PAC Type
(percentage)

	Quartile I	Quartile II	Upper Half	Quartile III	Quartile IV	Lower Half
1978						
Type I (ideological)	31.5	26.3	57.8	26.3	15.8	42.1
Type II (ideological leaning)	38.0	28.6	66.6	14.3	19.0	33.3
Type III (pragmatic leaning)	23.5	17.6	41.1	23.5	35.3	58.8
Type IV (pragmatic)	0.0	25.0	25.0	37.5	37.5	75.0
1980						
Type I (ideological)	46.7	13.3	60.0	26.7	10.0	40.0
Type II (ideological leaning)	17.0	39.0	56.0	22.0	22.0	44.0
Type III (pragmatic leaning)	25.0	12.5	37.5	25.0	37.5	62.5
Type IV (pragmatic)	15.0	25.0	40.0	25.0	35.0	60.0

tion for 1980 by PAC type, the following results appear: Type I (fifteen) $90,383; Type II (twenty-three) $61,029; Type III (eight) $46,723; Type IV (twenty) $48,297.

A relationship between size of PAC and tendency to be ideological or pragmatic in giving appears in the data. Such indications are supported by observations repeatedly made by PAC officers in interviews, especially by officers of pragmatic or pragmatic-leaning PACs. Where the PAC raises quite limited amounts of money and its representative notes that its fund raising is "paltry" or "hand-to-mouth," it will feel obliged to channel such money as it has into contributions to support key incumbents in districts where the corporation has significant locations. These will be the incumbents with whom the PAC needs to maintain an established relationship or whose past constituency services it wants to recognize. When the contributions such modest-sized PACs believe they must make to incumbents are made, there may be little venture capital left to devote to the support of challengers, especially in districts where a corporation does not have its own plant locations. In addition, PACs that are experiencing trouble in raising money tend to have a lower sense of political efficacy; that is, they are likely to be skeptical about their ability to be an important force for political change. On the other hand, PACs that have turned ideological or ideological leaning are usually raising enough money so that a surplus remains for risk taking after the must donations have been made to a minimum of incumbents. Their superior fund-raising performance seems also to be associated with greater confidence in their capability to have impact on the political process.

2. The role of the Washington representative: In a letter to fellow members of the Business Roundtable, widely circulated in PAC circles, Donald M. Kendall of Pepsico expressed astonishment at the apparent trends of corporate-PAC giving in the 1978 election. At the time (September 1978), incomplete data indicated that most corporate-PAC giving was going to incumbents, and heavily to Democrats. (Later data showed a major shift to challengers and Republicans in the last weeks of the campaign.) Kendall offered an explanation: "I cannot help wondering whether this might not be a function of the, in my opinion, inflated roles Washington representatives of some companies play in picking recipients of PAC funds."[15] In this view, the Washington representative has a primary focus of interest in maintaining access to incumbents with whom he has already established relationships. The normal expectation is, therefore, that where the Washington representative has major or decisive influence in recommending candidates to receive contributions, the likely result is a pragmatically oriented PAC; where his influence is negligible, an ideological PAC is the more probable outcome.

By one estimate, 250 corporations now maintain Washington offices, with an average of ten new ones being opened annually.[16] The scope of functions of the Washington office varies according to whether it is the primary site of the corporation's government-relations activity or whether it shares such responsibilities with a government-relations department at corporate headquarters. The Washington representative, whether a registered lobbyist or not, will try to bring to bear on politicians the corporate position on significant issues affecting its interests. Washington representatives function, as one of them put it, as the "in-house politicians" of their corporations. Increasingly they are recruited directly out of the political world. Washington representatives have had an important role in initiating PACs, as they have felt the need for funds to respond to invitations to fund-raising affairs of congressmen. They are often officers of PACs and are a key source of information and recommendations, primarily about incumbents, in candidate-support decisions.

For forty-one of the PACs in the sample it was possible to collect detailed enough data about the role of the Washington representative to allow inferences with a high probability of accuracy about their influence in PAC decisions. In seventeen cases, the influence of the representative was minor or negligible; in fourteen of these cases, (80 percent), the PACs were ideological (I-II) and in three, (20 percent), they were pragmatic (III-IV). Of twenty-four PACs where the representative's influence was major or decisive, fifteen were pragmatic, (63 percent), and nine were ideological, (37 percent).

These figures are consistent with the Kendall proposition. More often than not, where major influence of a Washington representative is present, a pragmatic PAC appears. Overwhelmingly, where such influence is negligible, an ideological PAC is likely. It would be a mistake, however, to think that the absence of Washington-representative influence suffices to produce an ideological PAC. This would amount to saying that the normal tendency of corporate PACs is to run in an ideological direction, unless deflected by the Washington representative. The hypothesis is most helpful in explaining the behavior of the not negligible number of PACs established on Washington-representative initiative and for the purpose of providing funds to respond to congressional fund raisers. The presence or absence of the influence of the Washington representative, although an important variable, is not sufficient in itself to explain the direction of PAC giving. A fuller explanation must be sought in more deeply rooted variables.

3. Degree of corporate diversification: In a major article on campaign finance, Michael Malbin distinguished between general-interest and special-interest PACs. The former use contributions to help politicians that are broadly probusiness; the latter are "defensive givers" who are more likely to seek to influence policy relating to a particular line of business. This special interest-general interest dichotomy corresponds to the ideological-

pragmatic distinction adopted in this work. Malbin argues that the special-interest focus appears among PACs whose corporations have economic interests concentrated in a single industry, and that the general interest orientation appears among PACs whose corporations have broader, more diverse economic interests. Degree of corporate diversification of economic activity is considered to be the main influence on the direction of PAC giving.[17]

The hypothesis was tested for PACs in the sample by comparing the degree of diversification between ideological and pragmatic PACs. By means of the Standard Industrial Classification (SIC) index, the parent corporations were classified as undiversified (single industry), minimally diversified (two industries), moderately diversified (three industries), and highly diversified (four or more industries). The results are summarized in table 2-6.

Both a higher incidence of diversification and higher levels of such diversification appear among the ideological PACs. However, important diversification, even if in lesser degree, appears among the pragmatic PACs.

Some intraindustry comparisons were also run. In the oil industry, for example, where the PACs are uniformly ideological, this was found to occur despite the fact that oil companies vary in degree of diversification. In the transportation sector (airlines and rails), the PACs are uniformly pragmatic, and this appears even though the companies vary from undiversified to highly diversified. The data provide some limited corroboration of the Malbin hypothesis, but do not lend support to the view that diversification is by itself a sufficient explanation of PAC variation. The results of intraindustry comparisons, in particular, suggest that some more deeply rooted influences are at work. Despite diversification, the typical large-scale corporation makes the bulk of its sales in some single industry (or closely related industries), and the behavior of its PAC is influenced primarily by the outlook and requirements of that industry.

4. Industrial or nonindustrial character of the parent corporation: Corporate PACs in the sample have been drawn from both the industrial and

Table 2-6
Corporate Diversification and PAC Type

Degree of Diversification	Number in Sample	Ideological PACs		Pragmatic PACs	
		Number	Percentage	Number	Percentage
Undiversified (1)	19	8	42	11	58.0 = 100
Minimally diversified (2)	8	7	87.5	1	12.5 = 100
Moderately diversified (3)	8	5	62.5	3	37.5 = 100
Highly diversified (4 or more)	30	20	66.7	10	33.3 = 100

nonindustrial sectors. It seems appropriate, therefore, to test whether contribution strategies differ in any marked degree between PACs in these two broad sectors of our economic life. The data are summarized in table 2-7.

Two out of three of the sample PACs formed by industrial corporations are either ideological or ideological leaning in orientation. On the other hand, almost two out of three of the PACs sponsored by nonindustrial corporations are pragmatic or pragmatic leaning. The data demonstrate significant differences in the direction of giving between corporate PACs in the two sectors. Among the nonindustrials, rails, airlines, banks, utilities, and financials lean more definitely to the pragmatic side than do building and construction or retailing.

5. Regulatory environments: There can be little quarrel with the proposition that the growth of federal regulatory activity has proceeded to the point of major generalized impact on the corporate world. Nevertheless, it is equally true that there are important distinctions to be made concerning the nature and character of the specific government-business interface that prevails in different industries and sectors of the economy. A major position taken in this study is that there is a variety of regulatory environments within which corporations interact with government, and that these differing environments constitute the most powerful influence in generating variation in PAC strategies. Furthermore, the previously noted broad differentiation in contribution orientation prevailing between industrial and nonindustrial PACs can be shown to be related in turn to differences in the regulatory environments in which industrials and nonindustrials operate. A significant convergence appears between hypotheses (5) and (4) that inferentially includes (3) as well. Five types of regulatory environment will be distinguished, and the relationship indicated between each type and PAC orientation:

1. The key features of the first environment are corporations in industries with long-standing, and, on the whole, acquiescent and comfortable relationships with one or more industry-specific federal agency with wide scope of authority and committees of both Houses exercising agency oversight and dealing with an agenda of legislative issues that centrally affects the well-being of the enterprises concerned. Sixty percent of all pragmatic or pragmatic-leaning PACs in the sample are affiliated with nonindustrial corporations that operate in this type of environment. Included are PACs in railroads, airlines, banks, and, to a lesser extent, utilities and financials. (Although some deregulation has taken place, and more may be in prospect, some firms in these industries opposed such measures: in any case, despite partial deregulation, these industries remain in fact among the more heavily regulated in the American economy.) These PACs direct their contributions primarily to the

Table 2-7
Industrial or Nonindustrial Activity and PAC Type

PAC Type	I		II		III		IV		Indeterminate	
	Number	*Percentage*	*Number*	*Percentage*	*Number*	*Percentage*	*Number*	*Percentage*	*Number*	*Percentage*
Industrials (1978)	17	36.0	15	32.0	7	15.0	3	6.0	5	11.0
(1980)	12	26.0	19	40.0	6	13.0	7	15.0	3	6.0
Nonindustrials (1978)	2	8.0	6	25.0	10	42.0	5	21.0	1	4.0
(1980)	3	13.0	4	17.0	2	8.0	13	54.0	2	8.0

maintenance of access to incumbents who are members of the key over-sight committees. Democrats, including liberals, receive a significant part of their funds.

2. In the second type of government-business interface, the corporation typically is in quest of positive action, or a continuation of favorable action, on its behalf, as a condition of well-being and viability. The positive state is in a position to withhold or dispense favors, benefits, or largesse. The corporations may be competing for government business or asking for insulation in some form from market forces. Twenty-five percent of all pragmatic or pragmatic-leaning PACs in the sample are affiliated with industrial corporations that fall within this regulatory environment. Typical instances are a defense contractor; a company needing a loan guarantee for survival; a company heavily engaged in research and development projects supported by the federal govern-ment; a company that asks for "Buy American" provisions requiring preferential government procurement of domestic products; a company needing protection against foreign competitors. In 1980 an important shift in contribution strategy in a pragmatic direction was taken by the Big Three in the auto industry. The distresses of the industry led its ma-jor firms to seek a variety of forms of government relief; incumbent Democrats (liberal and labor oriented) have been more supportive allies in the quest for relief than free-market conservative Republicans.

3. Over 50 percent of all ideological or ideological-leaning PACs in the sample (excluding the oil related) are affiliated with industrial corpora-tions that are reacting to an intensive experience of the impact of a mul-tiplicity of new regulatory agencies (Occupational Safety and Health Administration, Environmental Protection Agency, Equal Employ-ment Opportunity Commission), and the reinvigoration of old ones (Federal Trade Commission). The new agencies are functional in char-acter, and economy-wide in scope. Corporate relationships with these agencies are still in the process of evolution and definition, and cor-porate discomfort with many of their decisions and actions runs high. Analysis of the costs and benefits of their activities has reinforced the corporate conviction that the impact, on the whole, on the business system has been adverse, contributing to problems of inflation, unemployment, lagging productivity, and declining competitiveness. The ideological PACs reflect their parent corporations' belief that altering the unfavorable climate for business created by the new regula-tion requires priority of emphasis in campaign giving on securing change in the political direction of Congress.

4. In the seventies the pressures of the continuing energy crisis created a special regulatory environment for the oil industry. The frustrations of chronic shortages and rising prices, in the midst of an unresolved debate

about appropriate energy policy, brought out high levels of public disapproval and suspicion. No other industry has recently been the target of so many legislative proposals for restriction, for regulatory alternatives to the free market, even for fundamental restructuring. A sense of threat in the industry has been reflected in the stance of its PACs. Thirty-five percent of all the ideological or ideological-leaning PACs in the sample are affiliated with oil-related industrials. Among corporate PACs they are the most consistent adherents, as a group, of a strategy of devoting the major share of PAC funds to support of conservative challengers.

5. An officer of a pragmatic PAC, replying to criticisms of ideological PACs about excessive support of incumbents, observed that "the further the government is from you from day to day, the more ideological you can afford to be." He was calling attention to the existence of still another regulatory environment: Despite the general impact of federal regulation, there are companies and industries that do not face immediate issues involving them directly with the federal government and that, therefore, do not have a day-to-day interest to be upheld in Washington. Some corporations in this environment have elected not to have PACs at all. Others, particularly if led by strong personalities with intense free-enterprise convictions, have been the home ground of pure ideological PACs.

Conclusion

Students of corporate political behavior have diverged sharply in their perceptions of the extent of political diversity or homogeneity to be encountered in the corporate sector. One polarity in this debate finds an absence of single mindedness and unity of purpose a central attribute of the aggregate political activity of large-scale business. In this view, there is reason to doubt whether, politically speaking, a corporate community can realistically be deemed even to exist. On the other hand, one of the more distinguished former expositors of a pluralistic view of American politics has urged more recently that business "tends to speak in one voice" and that large corporations, although perhaps differing on secondary matters, approach a consensus on what he designates as the grand issues of politics.[18]

This debate has additional significance because of the clear relationship between positions on corporate political diversity and views of the extent of corporate political influence. Those who stress the importance of the political diversity in the corporate world view it as a major self-limiting control on the exercise of effective corporate political influence, and consequently, as an indispensable contributor to the maintenance of pluralism in politics. Those who emphasize the political cohesion of American business have also been prone to call attention to what they regard as the uniquely influential and indeed privileged position of American businessmen in our politics.[19]

Examination of contribution strategy reveals no pattern to which PACs uniformly adhere. Instead, two mainstreams of PAC giving are discernible, and within each of these streams are varying degrees of consistency with which the dominant ideological or pragmatic trend is followed. In a comparative view, the diversity among corporate PACs is much greater than that found among labor PACs, which in 1978 and 1980 made over 90 percent of their contributions to candidates of one party. However, it goes too far to maintain that the diversity among PACs is sufficiently extensive to support the view that, in a political sense, there is no business community. Cohesion appears in the wide prevalence among PACs of free-enterprise sentiments, as expressed in their solicitation literature and statements of purpose. Shared political preferences among pragmatic and ideological PACs appear also in decisions to support challengers. Although pragmatic PACs focus heavily on incumbents, their behavior is similar to the ideological PACs when they do elect to support challengers. They are, then, as little likely as the ideological PACs to support other than conservatives, Republicans or Sunbelt Democrats. Pragmatic PACs may back liberal Democratic incumbents for access purposes, but rarely will they support a liberal Democratic challenger.

Despite this evidence of shared political sentiments, corporate PACs express differences in priorities and perceived interests in a continuum of contribution strategies. A number of factors were found to correlate with the dispersion in PAC giving. Pragmatic PACs, when compared with ideological PACs, had parent corporations that were relatively less diversified in structure and more often nonindustrial in their dominant economic activity. Students of the government-business relationship distinguish between the traditional industry-specific, old regulation and the new social regulation that crosses industry lines. Pragmatic PACs were more likely to be found in corporations affected by the old regulation, whereas ideological PACs were found more frequently among corporations in the orbit of the new regulation. PACs with a pragmatic tendency were also more likely to have parent corporations that did the most significant part of their business with the federal government, or that required some major form of government assistance to maintain viability. The divergence in PAC strategies may reflect as well some important nuances of difference within the conservative position generally espoused in the corporate community, between a centrist, moderate, accommodationist viewpoint and a much more "principled," intransigent New Right attitude. (This point is developed more fully in chapter 5.)

Some observers of the PAC phenomenon have speculated that the momentum of corporate-PAC growth presents a new kind of threat of corporate dominance of the political process. The evidence of a lack of single mindedness in corporate-PAC giving, however, points to the existence of at least one limitation on the potential for such dominance.

3 Corporate PACs as Fund Raisers

The question of whether or not the number of corporate PACs is likely to continue proliferating rapidly has been sharply argued by students of PACs.[1] However, another feature of PAC growth—their fund-raising capabilities—has received little attention. This is the more surprising in light of the fact that it is not only the number of PACs but also their ability to raise enough money that establishes political viability.

Professor Edwin M. Epstein likens present PAC numbers, political activities, and aggregate receipts to the tip of a possible iceberg. Most of the PAC potential for growth, lies hidden, but even the visible portion is impressive. Epstein notes that corporate PACs, whose approach to fund raising is "still at a rudimentary stage," collected $6.8 million from contributors in 1976, and $17.7 million in 1978. He believes that most PACs that have not yet implemented the kinds of solicitation policies that maximize revenues are moving in this direction through inclusion of many more managers, stockholders, and retirees, and through expenditure of the time, effort, and money needed to activate their growing constituencies. Fuller exploitation of PAC potential portends, in his opinion, continuation, in the 1980s, of exponential growth in aggregate incomes that corporate PACs enjoyed between 1976-1978.[2]

Former Congressman Clark MacGregor, chairman of the United Technologies PAC, takes exception to this view, asserting that "contributions to PACs are voluntary" and that the number of donors and the yields will not increase exponentially, especially since top management and boards of directors "go overboard in making absolutely sure that there is no coercion." While Epstein estimates that corporate PAC aggregate receipts will climb from the $17.7 million reached in 1978 to $40-50 million in 1982, MacGregor postulates that total annual receipts, when adjusted for inflation, will less than double between 1980 and 1985.[3]

PAC growth may take place through decisions by corporations to form new PACs and by internal growth (in funds available for campaign giving) of PACs already in being. This chapter deals with the latter dimension. (In chapter 4 prospects for growth in PAC numbers are considered.)

Once a PAC is established, there are three possible trajectories of internal growth: expansion of the number of exempts (executive or administrative personnel who have policymaking, managerial, professional, or supervisory responsibilities) whom the PAC elects to solicit; solicitation of constituencies other than exempts; and intensification of solicitation of exempts already in the solicitation universe. This intensification may occur through: changes in the method of solicitation (for example, supplement of letters with face-to-face contact); changes in the method of payment (for example, adoption of payroll deduction); more frequent solicitation; emphasis on guidelines as indicators of appropriate contribution levels; and utilization of a "hard sell" or pressure that falls short of the legal definition of coercion in the applicable statute (for example, solicitation of subordinates by superiors). This chapter examines what PACs are doing currently in each of the possible trajectories of growth, and also what they intend to do in the near future. It attempts to project, in broad terms, the potential for internal growth of PACs and to indicate which extrapolation, that of Epstein or of MacGregor, conforms more closely to the data. Whether the parameters of growth of corporate PACs are limited or indefinitely expandable has major implications for the controversy about potential corporate-PAC political influence.

Corporate-PAC Constituencies

The Exempts

Although they may legally seek financial support from hourly paid employees (under specified limitations) and stockholders, including retirees, corporate PACs concentrate fund-raising efforts on their management constituency. For the large-scale corporation, the number of people who qualify for consideration as management-level employees under the statutory definition is likely to run into the thousands. Corporate PACs, therefore, must decide at what levels of management they will direct their solicitation efforts; this is so important a decision in practice that the company CEO makes or approves it.

A first significant finding is that corporate PACs differ in important degree in the size of the management group they elect to solicit. Three categories of PACs may be distinguished in this regard: Category A PACs confine solicitation to the highest company officers; Category B PACs dip down as far as middle management; and Category C PACs include most or all exempts. Fourteen percent of the PACs in the sample fall into Category A; 47 percent into Category B; and 39 percent into Category C.

Category A PACs solicit an average of 152 managers, 101 of whom (67 percent) contribute at the rate of $288 per respondent, for a total of $29,088, to their fund. Category B PACs average 1,390 solicitees, nine times as many as the typical Category A PAC, with 316 (23 percent) giving an average $137. Increasing the number of solicitees leads to a drop in the rate of response and average contribution but still nets the typical Category B PAC $43,292, or 49 percent more dollars than the typical Category A PAC. The typical Category C PAC contacts 4,294 employees, 480 or 11 percent of whom give on the average $83, for a total of $39,480. This represents a return of 9 percent fewer dollars than the typical Category B PAC obtains, but 36 percent more than the typical Category A PAC total. (Response rates are based on data provided by sixty-nine PACs. Thirty-seven PACs furnished data on average contributions.)

For all PACs the size of the solicitation universe has important ramifications. Category A PACs, for example, prefer small numbers, because a highly selective constituency means a more manageable PAC and tighter control over the solicitation process. They deal with a small, tightly knit, loyal group of highly paid executives who have a large personal stake in the fortunes of their companies. Almost without exception, Category A PACs expect "to raise a high amount of money with a low-keyed effort," since they are dealing with the constituency most prone to support the company fund. Top managers are also discreet and reliable, unlikely to disagree with PAC political strategies or to resent importunings for money. One Category A PAC officer left no doubt as to why his committee does not tap the lower ranks: "You can expect dissidence from those at the $20,000-$25,000-and-below level whose points of view don't necessarily coincide with the company's. Their viewpoints might fall outside our guidelines and that would be a source of friction."

Category A PACs have quite thoroughly cultivated the limited numbers available at the executive-suite level. To increase revenues substantially they must either intensify the solicitation process, risking the antagonism of top-echelon employees who are already giving at very high rates, or solicit further down the managerial ladder. Thirty percent have decided to canvass the lower levels in 1980.

Category B PACs also are aware that extending eligibility to lower-level managers and doing more marketing of the PAC might increase revenues, but they are already raising more money, on the average, than those in the other two categories. There are other reasons for not soliciting lower levels, such as concern that a huge sum of money raised will hurt the company's public image. An interviewee explained: "A PAC needs enough money to help incumbents it wants to support and to help challengers and open seats. But too much money can give the impression of buying candidates."

Even those Category B PACs with poor returns hesitate to expand their constituency base. Some think that employee backlash is most likely to begin at the bottom level of management, where commitment to the company is less firm; others do not believe that solicitation at all levels will prove fruitful or cost effective.

The time, effort, and cost entailed in a Category C PAC's solicitation and record-keeping activities may not be justified in terms of monetary payoff. Diminishing returns apply to its total take as well as to its response rate and lower individual contribution. Despite a solicitation universe three times larger than that of a Category B PAC, its solicitations bring in less money. While it collects more money than the average Category A PAC, it canvasses a universe twenty-eight times larger. Category C PACs admit that disinterest and lack of adequate time devoted to the development of political awareness account for their relatively poor showing. Yet, despite the fact that support for PACs is strongest at the highest level and weakest at the lowest, 39 percent of the PACs in the sample have chosen to solicit most or all exempts, and this number is growing. Twenty percent of Category A PACs announced they were going to all levels in 1980. Category C PACs emphasize that, in addition to raising money, they want to raise the political consciousness of managerial employees. "Our philosophy," said an ideological PAC manager, "is to encourage a long-term undertaking and continuing involvement in the political process. We need politically active people who realize it is they who have to pay the bill for government mismanagement." A number of Category B and C PACs share this philosophy and have mounted extensive political education programs.

The Stockholders

A few years ago Irving Kristol argued forcefully that every institution needs a constituency, defined by him as a "substantial number of people who are loyal to the institution and who will rally to its defense when it is in trouble." Kristol urged that the managers of large publicly held corporations ought to regard stockholders as their natural constituency. He complained that managers were not doing enough to activate the potential of stockholders as allies and supporters. In fact, in recent years, a number of corporations have inaugurated or increased efforts to inform stockholders about their positions on pertinent public policy issues and have sought to enlist stockholders in grass-roots lobbying activities.[4]

Some provisions of the Federal Election Campaign Act represent acceptance by Congress of the idea that stockholders are a key political constituency of the corporations. The FEC in its SUN-PAC advisory opinion included stockholders among the groups that might be freely solicited by corporate PACs. Congress found the grant, in SUN-PAC, of solicitation rights too broad and made significant changes in this regard in the 1976 amendments, but it continued to include stockholders among the categories to whom corporate PACs could legitimately turn to raise their funds. The law even permits corporations to offer stockholders the option of contributing through dividend-deduction plans with the stipulation that corporations, on union request, may be required to make an equivalent option available to corporate rank-and-file employees who are union members and who may wish to contribute to the union's political fund.

One might have assumed that with a right to solicit stockholders legitimized by Congress, the number of corporate PACs drawing upon stockholders for funds, and the percentage of total funding contributed by stockholders would have expanded dramatically. To this point, however, such developments have conspicuously failed to materialize. A number of surveys of PAC practices—those by the Chamber of Commerce, Public Affairs Council, and the Conference Board—have shown that relatively few companies have so far ventured to approach stockholders for PAC contributions.[5] This study indicates that less than 20 percent of the companies queried carried out stockholder solicitations. An even more significant finding in some ways is that only a very few of those not engaging in solicitation of stockholders have definitely formulated plans to do so. Six percent indicated that the issue was under active consideration and review. Stockholder solicitation continues to be sparse among corporate PACs, and it does not show signs of catching on as an emerging trend. Although a number of PAC managers look longingly in this direction, they have not received the necessary approval from top management. They believe there is considerable potential among the stockholder population that they would like an opportunity to tap. One of them noted that, at the annual meeting, stockholders inquired of the CEO whether they might be permitted to contribute to the PAC. They were referred to the PAC manager. Yet this company has not made the decision to solicit stockholders formally.

For a number of reasons corporate leadership remains averse to authorization of stockholder solicitation. The most frequently mentioned explanation for the reluctance is doubt about the cost effectiveness of such solicitation. There is a widely shared conviction that the return from mass mailings (one must remember that we are considering corporations with thousands of individual stockholders) would not justify the considerable expense. Corporations bear the administrative costs of PAC activity, and most see little point in making expenditures from the corporate treasury for the PAC that would exceed income derived. There is not much disposition to expend some funds to test the market, to risk some corporate money to find out just how responsive stockholders might be, because there tends to be a heavy discount in advance of the possibilities. Most PAC spokesmen are also conscious that much work needs to be done to improve the effectiveness of solicitation of management-level employees within the firm before going far afield to approach stockholders. A low response rate from managers hardly helps make a case for stockholder solicitation.

For large corporations, the sheer mass and diversity of individual stockholders create uncertainty about their collective identity and doubts about receptiveness. Corporations may not be able to draw the profile of their stockholder population in exact terms. Many are transients with small holdings. Their attitudes on public questions of concern to the company may not be precisely known. Many have multiple affiliations and interests and do not approach the political process solely, or even predominantly, as owners. The owning of shares may not define one's politics. Many stockholders may be narrowly focused on maximizing their returns in the short run. They may respond to solicitations by insisting that corporations engaged in political activity are moving outside their appropriate sphere. It may be surmised that corporate leaders have equivocal feelings about activation of stockholders. When stockholders became active in the 1970s, it was as often to express alienation from management as to offer support and loyalty.

Because of the hesitancy of many corporations, the experience of the nine sample PACs that have tried stockholder solicitation is of particular interest. Eight of the nine follow an ideological trend in their campaign giving. Apparently, venturesomeness in supporting challengers and candidates for open seats, and militancy in seeking change in the political composition of Congress correlate positively with willingness to take risks in solicitation of funds as well. These companies act on the belief that stockholders have as much at stake as management in enhancing the capacity of business to protect its interests in relation to government. It is striking that energy or energy-related companies constitute over one-half of the group. Two of the companies solicit only from stockholders. In one case the PAC solicits employees, at all levels, who participate in its stock ownership plan, as well as outside stockholders. In the other case the PAC solicits a small number of top managers who are significant stockholders, and large shareholders who receive the major part of their income from such shares. Upper managers and the key stockholders are linked in this firm by strong personal ties.

Most report that returns have been sufficient to warrant continuation of their efforts. A cost-cutting method they find useful is the enclosure of a message about the PAC with dividend checks. Dividend deduction is encouraged. A two-percent return from a mass mailing is considered successful. One PAC, however, reported that returns had been disappointing, all the more so since the parent corporation had inaugurated a program to inform and motivate shareowners to engage in political action. Average contributions from stockholders for most of the group run considerably below the average for management-level employees. Among the stockholders the most likely to give are retirees or really large stockholders. A question as yet unresolved by the FEC is whether the solicitation of employee stockholders entitles a union to cross-solicitation rights. The absence of a clear FEC stand on this issue has inhibited some, but not all, PACs in the group from approaching employee stockholders. It should be noted that the companies that solicit receive some criticism from stockholders. Objectors may write to disagree with the contribution policies of the PAC (wrong candidates are being backed), or to express resentment that such rich companies try to raise money from them, or to raise doubts about the propriety of using stockholders' money for political purposes.

One company (here designated as company A) must be singled out for special attention because of the vigor and resourcefulness of its approach to stockholders. Company A built initially on some clues that its stockholders might be a willing political force waiting to be utilized. A survey of stockholder attitudes on a wide range of issues was carried out. Two results seemed promising: Over 80 percent of respondents said they wished to be informed about pertinent public issues and felt an obligation, when in agreement, to defend the company's position on such issues. Company A's PAC moved to solicit a mass of smaller shareholders and a small group of its largest shareholders. It has solicited over 40,000 shareholders, with holdings of at least 100 shares, by mail more than once, with a positive response rate of approximately two percent. A combination of telephone calls and personal letters by senior officers has been the method of addressing stockholders with several thousand shares. Here the positive response rate has been about 25 percent. The dividend-deduction option is permitted for all shareholders and is bringing in steady income for the PAC. Since there is no reason to suppose that company A's stockholders are unique, one must attribute its relative success to the creativity of its government-relations people strongly supported in their efforts by upper management.

A number of conclusions seem warranted on the basis of this examination of corporate PAC experience with stockholders. Such solicitation is not to be undertaken lightly. Careful preparation and an investment of time and money are required. Research into the shareholder population is advisable to find out who they are, identify their beliefs and attitudes, and locate the shareholder groups that constitute the loyal following of the corporation. One PAC, for example, is making an initial solicitation directed at stock-holding dealers whose identification with the corporation can be assumed to be strong. The most successful solicitations—those with greatest per capita returns—have been directed at these kinds of special stockholder groups. Stockholder employees, active and retired, have loyalties to the company that arise not from shareholding but from long association with the enterprise. Stockholders with large blocks of shares, who have held shares for a long time and who draw a significant part of their income from them, may identify with management and its problems with government and may be approached with confidence. (The small shareholder cannot be written off, however, because soliciting PACs report that they get some of their most heartening responses from stockholders who can afford to give only small amounts.)

Altogether, the experience thus far suggests that more might be done than has so far been attempted. But it does not indicate that stockholder contributions are likely, in the near future, to become a major source of PAC funding. Indeed the experience casts an equivocal light on the proposition that stockholders are the natural constituency of the corporation. The same kind of stockholder who reacts negatively to management expenditures for social-responsibility concerns, who detests public-interest stockholders' constant resolutions for disinvestment in South Africa, may respond negatively when management itself wants to raise money for political purposes. In practice, even though they are the owners of the enterprise, their numbers and diversity, the short-range nature of the concerns of many of them, their multiple affiliations, constitute difficulties in rallying them as an effective political constituency, and as a major source of corporate-PAC funding.

The Twice-Yearly Option

In 1976 when Congress moved a second time to revise the Federal Election Campaign Act it acted out of need to revise provisions of the law that had been invalidated in *Buckley* v. *Valejo*, but, in part, it also proceeded to amend, because of the largely unfavorable response to a key advisory opinion rendered by the FEC late in 1975. The Sun Company's PAC had requested an opinion on whom, exactly, it might solicit. The answer of the FEC's majority was a sweeping one: stockholders and *all* employees, with proper regard for the statutory provisions about avoidance of coercion. The opinion aroused major discontent among unions, who felt that the way was now open for management to compete with unions in raising political-action funds from hourly paid workers. Senior Democratic members of the Committee on House Administration expressed displeasure and asserted that the FEC, in the SUN-PAC opinion, had misread the intent of Congress.[6]

In 1976 in committee, on the floor, and in the conference committee of both houses, many hours were spent trying to hammer out an amendment that would satisfactorily revise the SUN-PAC opinion. What emerged from the deliberations and was duly enacted by Congress came to be called the twice-yearly option. Congress did not totally reject the idea that corporate PACs should have some solicitation access to hourly employees. A compromise was worked out that permits corporations and their PACs to solicit hourly paid employees twice a year by letter addressed to the home, while a reciprocal right was extended to unions and their PACs to solicit nonunion hourly paid employees, stockholders, and executives, with the same specified limitations. Furthermore, the amended law requires that a corporate PAC, intending to exercise the twice-yearly option, must give advance notice to the union with bargaining rights in the corporation, and must make available, at cost, the method used to reach the employees. The twice-yearly option was a satisfactory arrangement to most members of Congress because it seemed to give corporations and unions reciprocal access to the normal constituencies of one another on equal terms and under carefully explained limitations.[7]

If anyone in 1976 imagined that corporate PACs were anxious to extend solicitation to the blue-collar level, what has happened since adoption of the amendment should quickly disabuse him. Only a tiny percentage of the sample has chosen to exercise the option. Under 9 percent of the PACs have tried solicitation of nonexempt employees since 1976. Moreover, only 6 percent of them currently makes use of the option. The access to the hourly paid employees that the amended statute permits remains, for all practical purposes, unutilized by corporate PACs, and it is very clear why this is so. Consider that most PACs have made no move to approach stockholders; that over 60 percent of them confine their solicitation to upper-and-middle-management levels among the eligible employees. Since corporate PACs have not yet seen fit to cultivate these constituencies fully or at all, it is harldy surprising to find that they have not seriously contemplated the solicitation of their hourly paid workers. Most of the companies in the sample deal with one or more unions. The twice-yearly option would require the corporation to notify the union of its intent and to make available the method to be utilized. In simple terms, unionized companies are likely to avoid the option because it could invite a kind of retaliatory cross-over solicitation of nonunion employees (the most likely candidates), stockholders, and executives. It is at least a minor irony, after all the furor about the SUN-PAC advisory opinion and the hours of legislative time that were spent on fashioning an amendment that would be symmetrical in the opportunities for crossover, that, in fact, the twice-yearly option proved to be inviable. In a small way, this matter serves as another reminder that Congress and interest groups with special concerns about election-campaign legislation need to consider with great care the probable effects of proposed changes.

Soliciting Exempts

Methods of Solicitation

Next to its choice of which level of management to solicit, the most important decision a PAC makes in its capacity as a money producer is the method or combination of methods to use in solicitation; for just as there is a difference in the degree of support for PACs according to managerial rank canvassed, so, too, there is a difference in response rates (except for Category A PACs) that divides along a line of personal and impersonal contact with solicitees.

All PACs, of course, correspond with solicitees, but 60 percent of the sample use the mails to establish initial contact, than follow up with personal contact. For the remainder, however, the mails provide the sole point of contact. Some Category B and C PACs that solicit most of their constituents by mail use a person-to-person approach with top managers. (One PAC reported a ten-to-one response differential based on this two-level solicitation policy.) A few PACs tread a course somewhere between impersonal and personal, soliciting formally by letter and informally by direct contact.

Those establishing personal contact do so through one of five personal solicitation methods. First is the informal discussion approach. Second is the PAC-conducted group session, usually featuring an audio-visual presentation or speaker. At the conclusion, a PAC officer makes his sales speech in which he explains the purpose of the PAC and invites the members of the audience to join. Third is solicitation by PAC-trained employee volunteers. They are instructed to answer questions about the PAC and the rules of solicitation and are assigned twenty or so of their fellow managers to canvass. Four is the home-rule method used by some PACs soliciting nationwide. In order to keep the solicitation process in local hands, and thus maintain a personal bond between fund raisers and constituents, they delegate to presidents of subsidiary companies, division heads, plant managers, or PAC subcommittees, authority to decide solicitation policies in their territories. Local control is more personal, and it takes into account local issues. Thus, according to one interviewee, "It's more effective, because it has more meaning for the solicitees." Five is an eclectic approach, utilizing a combination of literature, audio-visual devices, and oral communication. Few PACs, as yet, use this approach, some because it raises possible legal, administrative, and public-relations problems; others because solicitation requires time and people and this costs money.

None of the five face-to-face methods of solicitation stands out from the others in terms of its response rate; but when their results are compared collectively to those attained by mail, the difference is marked.

Half of the Category B PACs solicit by mail only, a surprisingly large proportion since this method elicits, on the average, a relatively poor 16 percent response as compared to the 29 percent average that those using some form of personal contact net. Returns from Category C PACs follow the same pattern. Fifty-six percent communicate by mail only, bringing a sparse 9-percent return, whereas those soliciting face to face average 16 percent, again a nearly two-to-one differential. Method, not level, determines the different response rates within each category. However, the data also show a nearly two-to-one differential between Category B and C PACs using the same methods (16 percent to 9 percent for mail-only solicitation and 29 percent to 16 percent for personal-contact solicitation). In this case, differences in numbers and levels of management solicited account for the disparity.

Category B PACs, using only the mails, average 1,700 solicitees; those employing face-to-face methods 1,360, a not disproportionate difference.

For many of them, choice of method, like choice of level, is governed by concern about consequences. They want to avoid the United Way approach of assessing a percentage of gross income. They are, if anything, overzealous in avoiding solicitation practices that could bring regulatory pressure down upon them. Others mention "the Watergate attitude" or express fear that if they become more aggressive in solicitation they will court public disfavor.

For Category C PACs the problem of numbers reaches another dimension. Those that solicit by mail only contact on the average 7,400 managers; those that contact solicitees face to face, 2,700. Solicitation of thousands of employees imposes logistical constraints that do not apply to PACs more selective in whom they solicit.

Category A PAC response rates are not affected by method of solicitation. They bring high returns regardless of method because they concentrate on an elite constituency. Their success results entirely from whom and not how they solicit.

No Category A PAC mentioned any plan to change its method of solicitation. Thirty-one percent of the mail-only Category B PACs, bowing to the logic that mail solicitation draws only one contributor for every two brought in by face-to-face methods, intend to switch to a personal approach. Twenty-three percent of the Category C PACs using the mails alone also plan to change. Nevertheless, for PACs soliciting thousands of exempts, mail remains the most practical method of reaching the multitude. For them, in their choice of solicitation method at least, numbers are destiny.

Guidelines

In accordance with the law, PACs assure solicitees that size of contribution is a personal choice that will neither hinder nor favor an employee's career or status with the company. Although some, as a gesture to employee feelings, refrain from setting any expectations, most provide benchmarks for giving. In some cases these take the form of an acceptable minimum donation or the $5,000 maximum allowable by law. (Minima vary from $25 to $250 per year; maxima from $100 to the $5,000 limit.) More often, PACs provide detailed indicators of what is considered a fair donation.

Seventy percent of Category A PACs furnish solicitees with guidelines for donations, ranging from one-half of 1 percent to 1 percent of gross annual income. Sixty-one percent of Category B PACs fix their guidelines between ¼ and 1 percent. Twenty-one percent use a sliding-scale guideline pegged to salary level, a method more popular in middle and lower echelons because of respective salaries. Fifty-seven percent of Category C PACs suggest contributions of between ¼ and 1 percent of income. Twenty-nine percent use the sliding-scale guideline.

Guidelines in all three categories remain suggestions that most contributors fail to follow. Top managers contribute on the average $288 which, if it were 1 percent of salary, would mean a $28,800 income; for middle managers the $137 average contribution would come from a $13,700 salary; and for those in the lower echelons the $83 average contribution would mean an annual income of $8,300. Even if projected from one-half of 1 percent, the resultant salary figures are not realistic. Obviously, donations reflect more the salary level then approximations of PAC guidelines based on salary.

Frequency of Solicitation

Surprisingly, PACs with many more managers to contact show a higher frequency of solicitation. One-third of Category B PACs, 37 percent of Category C PACs, and less than 1 percent of Category A PACs solicit more than once a year. The reason for the discrepancy is that Category A PAC solicitors know most, if not all, top managers whom they solicit for contributions, and a single contact, even if by letter, elicits a high response. Even though PACs in the other two categories have to reach hundreds or even thousands of middle-and-lower level managers, their low response rates may prompt them to more than one solicitation.

Although more solicitations might increase revenues, only a minority of PACs in the sample conduct more than one solicitation per year. For the great majority, the risk of giving offense to employees outweighs financial considerations. Top managements want successful PACs, but they do not want this goal pursued so single mindedly that it results in deteriorating employee morale.

Payroll Deduction

Corporate PACs make alternative methods of payment available to contributors. Some allow only a single lump-sum payment by check; a few utilize pledging, allowing employees to fulfill the pledge by payments over several months; in some instances monthly billing is used. But increasingly, payroll deduction, an option specifically permitted by the Federal Election Campaign Act, has gained ground. Sixty percent of the PACs in the sample have already adopted payroll deduction, and an additional 12 percent have received top management authorization to institute it. Most PACs that have made it available find that it soon becomes the most popular option and that it accounts for the larger part of the funds raised. A number of PACs frankly encourage and recommend it. For PACs that solicit at executive levels below top management, payroll deduction is helpful. Senior managers may prefer to pay by check, but deciding to give is apparently rendered less painful at lower levels by payroll deduction.

The advantage of payroll deduction most frequently mentioned by PAC spokesmen is stabilization of the number of contributors. It is widely viewed as the best way to sustain support for the PAC. The money comes in regularly, and even in off-election years when solicitation is most difficult. Payroll deduction has continuity, that is, once an employee has authorized it, deductions go on being made automatically and without time limit, unless the employee withdraws authorization in writing. Cancellation has to be initiated by the employee. Resolicitation of such contributors may not be necessary every year, although, in practice, the PAC may want to approach contributors to urge them to increase their deductions. One PAC reported that, since 1977, it has not carried out any solicitations; with payroll deduction the flow of income from a single solicitation has been sufficient for its requirements.

The manager of one of the more successful PACs in the country stated frankly that payroll deduction was a necessity for his operation. It made possible effective planning and implementation of a coherent campaign donation strategy. The regular cash flow provided early money for entering primaries and for contributions through the whole campaign. Without it, money in sufficient amounts could not be raised in off-election years. In an election year, without payroll deduction it would be relatively late, after interest in outcomes has peaked, before the PAC could raise enough funds to make significant contributions.

Some PACs that have recently adopted payroll deduction have done so after a rather painful experience of erosion in number of contributors. In one case almost two-thirds of the PAC contributors were new in 1978, and a majority of those contributing in 1976 had dropped out. The expectation is that payroll deduction will forestall this kind of turnover and also reduce frequency of solicitations. But payroll deduction does not always raise an effective barrier against PAC erosion. Three companies report that large turnover of contributors has taken place despite payroll deduction. Clearly, when executive-level employees have some impelling motivation to cease giving, they will not be inhibited from doing so by the continuous feature. For example, one of the three companies, fallen on hard times, cut back sharply on executive bonuses. Executives responded by cancellation of payroll deduction for the PAC. A 30 percent drop in contributions occurred over two years.

Among PACs with payroll deduction, concerns are expressed on two points. The continuous feature, despite its advantages, inspires some misgivings. One PAC officer believes that the FEC has given tacit consent to the continuous feature; nevertheless, his PAC provides that payroll deduction for contributors cease after one year, unless the contributor authorizes continuance. The burden is put on the PAC to obtain renewal of consent. Payroll deduction also raises the issue of possible violation of the anonymity of givers and nongivers, because it requires that at least a minimum of persons in the payroll department know which employees are on the register. Sensitivity on this point has led one company, in its PAC literature, to explain that payroll deduction means that the individuals in the payroll department will know the identity of givers, but then a strong statement from the CEO is quoted that makes clear that payroll department employees who reveal names of individuals on the register could face disciplinary action.

A minority of companies (28 percent) remains opposed to payroll deduction, even though the matter has come up for consideration, in some instances more than once. Significant objections to it, centering in the legal, personnel, or industrial relations departments, continue to be persuasive to top management, and there are PAC managers who oppose it. The objectors seem to read the election campaign statute more stringently than does the FEC itself. Some see payroll deduction as intrinsically coercive, as involving too much force. The automatic feature of payroll deduction is considered an impairment of freedom of choice. Giving, it is believed, ought always to be the result of a conscious choice. The most frequently cited ground of opposition, however, is the opinion that it is incompatible with anonymity. This is seen to outweigh any compensating advantages: "There should be a Chinese wall on information about who gives and doesn't."

The remaining objections of the PACs refraining from adopting payroll deduction may be summarized briefly. Some PAC officers believe that it is not necessarily an effective inducement. Employees may feel that there are already too many deductions from their pay, and they may decide to set limits. There may be resentment to an additional proposed deduction that further increases the already wide disparity between gross and net income. PACs that confine solicitation to the highest management levels may disdain payroll deduction as unnecessary. The collection process for such executives can be kept simple and administrative costs minimized. Very high income people do not need it to stimulate and sustain their giving. As one PAC officer commented: "Our contributors are able to write checks. We don't need payroll deduction for the level we solicit." One company thinks of the PAC as akin to a voluntary outside organization. It permits payroll deduction for only one such organization, the United Fund. In this way it avoids having to yield to possible requests from a variety of voluntary organizations to use payroll deduction. Industrial relations managers have effectively opposed payroll deduction for PAC contributors in labor relations situations where a company may be resisting union efforts to obtain the checkoff. Industrial relations officers in two companies believe that allowing payroll deduction for the PAC would undermine management's case against the checkoff. Finally it should be noted that a few strong-minded officers of effective PACs oppose payroll deduction out of a concern with the quality of the act of giving. In this respect they are rather like some business agents of local unions who prefer not to rely on a checkoff, because they think it makes dues collection automatic and creates remoteness in relations between union leaders and rank and file. Such PAC officers believe that giving should be an affirmative action, reflecting the involvement and commitment of the giver. A successful PAC ought not to have to depend on payroll deduction. It should be able to rely on the positive responses of executives that understand their own stake in what the PAC is trying to accomplish.

Given that it is sanctioned by law and that it is useful in sustaining giving, payroll deduction not surprisingly has spread quickly to over two-thirds of the PACs in the sample. It would be a mistake, however, to think that payroll deduction by itself could turn a PAC into a successful fund raiser. Some of the more successful PACs have done nicely without it, and it has not prevented erosion where negative factors were present and working to undermine interest. What ultimately sustains giving is a state of mind that payroll deduction by itself has little to do with creating. A minority of PACs continues to reject payroll deduction on a number of counts. Residual opposition is likely to persist, especially among the PACs whose objections are grounded in concerns about possible violations of employee rights.

Anonymity

PACs typically pursue policies designed to protect the privacy of the decision whether or not to support the fund. They keep to a minimum the number of company employees who have access to fund records, and those who keep the records are under strict orders not to betray this confidence. No employee is supposed to ask for or give information about contributions. Any violation of the anonymity of solicitees can bring immediate termination. A PAC that abridges the privacy of an employee's decision on participation runs the risk of offending contributors and noncontributors alike.

PACs that fail to seal off records from potentially interested parties are not necessarily at fault. Employees who collect and administer PAC receipts (usually the PAC treasurer, his clerical assistants, and selected payroll department personnel), are privy to information on contributions and are enjoined by superiors not to divulge information, except as required by law. However, the possibilities for security leaks, given the human condition, are manifest.

Concern about employee access to records translates into concern about possible breaches of anonymity. So strong are the apprehensions of some PACs on this score that they eschew the advantages of payroll deduction on the grounds that, by limiting the number of employees who know who is or is not giving, they are reducing the risk of leakage.

Some PACs carry their attempts to quarantine privileged information a step farther. A few bypass the company's legal department in favor of an independent legal firm to review fund activities. A more common procedure is to engage the services of a bank as trustee of contributions; thus only outsiders handle the accounting procedures.

In spite of such precautions, it is unlikely that a PAC, however sincere its efforts, can devise a fail-safe system of security. Federal law requires all PACs to file periodic reports with the FEC containing the names, addresses, occupations, and the amount of the donation of everyone who gives more than $100 or who earmarks a contribution of any size. In turn, the FEC files on PACs are subject to public disclosure. Entangled in this legal thicket is a "Catch-22" paradox: Although companies try to guarantee that the privacy of a solicitee's choice will be inviolate, any interested party can uncover the names of those who contributed (or did not contribute) $100 or more to a specific fund simply by consulting FEC records.

Coercion and Pressure

The intent of Congress in federal electoral law was to shield corporate employees from coercive PAC solicitation practices. The law stipulates that contributions are not to be secured by threat or use of force, job discrimination, or financial reprisal. PACs must inform solicitees of the purpose of the fund. In addition, solicitees must be told that guidelines for giving are suggestions, not requirements, and that the decision whether to give or not will not affect conditions of employment.[8] Beyond these requirements, however, the law and FEC regulations are vague or even silent on the question of just how much pressure PACs may apply, although debates preceding adoption afford additional clues of congressional intent. Fund raisers, then, are relatively free to use whatever degree of pressure they deem necessary, so long as they do not violate the specific provisions of the law. That most PACs raise relatively modest sums suggests that considerations other than filling their coffers play a part in their solicitation practices.

Concern for the sensibilities of solicitees has even led a few companies to provide ombudsmen to handle grievances that might arise from PAC operations. Other companies urge solicitees to bring complaints to the company's legal department. If an offended employee prefers not to use company channels, he may submit his complaint to the FEC for disposition. Information about the number of employee complaints is not available, since it is FEC policy not to publicize cases of alleged coercion at the investigative stage. The FEC would reveal the particulars only if an adverse finding were made; and, thus far, the FEC has made no such finding. Although FEC policy might seem an open invitation to PACs to adopt more zealous fund-raising techniques, PAC officers assert that PAC caution is legal caution and that, if anything, PACs are "overly stringent in their adherence to the law."

However, the FEC has made a ruling on a suit brought in 1979 by the International Association of Machinists and others against eleven corporate PACs, alleging that their "solicitation of mid-level career managers and professionals for contributions to separate segregated funds are inherently coercive, resulting in non-voluntary contributions." The complainants charged: failure to protect the anonymity of contributors; use of supervisors to conduct person-to-person solicitations; refusal to permit contributors to designate their funds by party or by candidate; and orchestration of the amounts of employee contributions as evidenced by the extraction of contributions from the great majority of their solicitees in amounts beyond normal giving.

The FEC ruled against the complainants, stating that even if all the allegations were proven (which the FEC did not feel was the case) they did not constitute violation of the Federal Election Campaign Act.[9] In short, coercion, as defined by law, is illegal; but the use of pressure in the selling of the PAC is not.

Critics of the corporate-PAC movement, like the International Association of Machinists, maintain that all managerial solicitees are subject to pressure "because of the inherently coercive nature of the employer-employee relationship." As former Congressman John Anderson stated: "Whether or not it [the individual's contribution to the PAC] is wholly voluntary depends, I suppose, on who asks whom for a contribution."[10] If a senior executive personally approaches a subordinate for a contribution, it is understandable if the solicitee feels a sudden urge to contribute. For pressure to be effective, method of solicitation also must be considered. A solicitation letter signed by the CEO gets poor results, but the CEO who buttonholes managers in his office is bound to be a successful fund raiser.

Although downhill solicitation is permissible under FEC regulations, standard PAC policy is to guard against superior-subordinate solicitation. Some have argued that any contact is synonymous with pressure. Although it is true that Category B and Category C PACs using personal contact outperform those using the mails only, one PAC which solicits 40,000 shareholders (not subject to the employer-employee relationship) reports rates that diverge even more sharply than do the returns from exempts, according to method and level of solicitation. Only 2 percent of the smaller shareholders respond favorably to an impersonal solicitation letter. The response rate from the largest shareholders, those receiving personal letters and follow-up phone calls from high company officials, is an impressive 25 percent.

The corporate-PAC movement is operating in the aftermath of Watergate and a spate of revelations concerning alleged illicit corporate-campaign contributions. Most corporate leaders who sanctioned the establishment of PACs transmit a sense of caution about money matters. Corporate legal- and public-affairs officers have added their voices to those decisionmakers who warn about the dangers of a hard-sell policy. They are apprehensive that those PACs that bend the law in the quest for huge revenues are likely to threaten the existence of the entire corporate-PAC movement. Policies of conscription would eventually outrage both solicitees and the general public. This could lead to legal challenges and unfavorable publicity, or spur Congress into adopting remedial measures.

There are corporate PACs that are based on the belief that money is an absolutely essential part of any political endeavor and that the more intense the cultivation of solicitees the better the chances for good returns. Several PAC managers expressed surprise that the FEC has not yet ruled against certain overzealous PACs for badgering solicitees. In their opinion those who use the Bond Drive and United Fund approach to wring money out of employees "are playing with fire." A few companies, however, are willing to run the risk. One is engaged in a crusade to consolidate corporate PACs along ideological lines. This company preaches that pressure is the ultimate persuader in any sales effort, and, beyond observing the voluntary requirements on giving, it is both legal and sound policy "to sell as hard as they know how the benefits that a PAC can provide in the elective process." The CEO of this company evidently follows his own advice. He is quoted as having said: "If they don't give they get a sell."[11] Not surprisingly, this company's PAC has by far the highest average individual contribution among the seventy-one in the sample.

Motivations of Noncontributors

PAC officers, like fund raisers in many voluntary organizations, are likely to become expert on the subject of why there are so many noncontributors. The percentages of negative response among eligible exempts run high. Among PACs that solicit top management exclusively (where identification with the enterprise is strongest) only one out of three on the average is a nongiver; but among PACs that solicit both top and middle management, three out of four are nongivers; and among PACs that solicit most or all eligibles nine out of ten on the average do not contribute. Because PAC officers want to increase the number of contributors and the overall amounts collected, they are particularly interested in gaining an understanding of the outlook of the noncontributors as a basis for devising strategies to improve fund-raising performance. In a variety of ways, through informal channels, and because some noncontributors do not hesitate to say what is on their minds, PAC officials have an opportunity to gain insight into their attitudes. Some officers report at least a trickle of mail, usually, but not always, unsigned, in which noncontributors react to solicitation efforts. In one instance twenty seven such letters were received.

What follows is a summary of the perceptions of PAC spokesmen about why eligible employees fail to contribute:

Nongivers hold negative attitudes toward politics and politicians; they see the latter as a "bunch of crooks." They are drawn to the "politics stinks syndrome." The notion that one can participate meaningfully in politics by helping to fund campaigns is a foreign idea. Some are sure that such giving means buying votes and that it contributes to already high levels of political corruption. They do not easily relate the future of their corporation and their own future to what happens in the political arena. There seems to be a lack of alertness to their role as citizens. A number of PAC officers in high-technology firms agree that scientists, technicians, and engineers are among the most negative in their responses: "Politics is not the 'bag' of technical people." One spokesman observed that some of the best business minds in his company were "abysmally ignorant, juvenile even" about politics. They were persons of "narrow interests and focus," whose management tasks absorbed their entire time. Even as they take note of political inertness among managers, PAC officers, especially if they are public-affairs professionals, express a self-critical conviction that they need to do a better job of helping exempts to see why it is important to be part of the political process.

Nongivers are by no means all politically apathetic or cynical. Some are armed with philosophical convictions. They may insist that funding of political campaigns is not a proper role for the corporation, that it ought to stick to its own business. Some prefer to give as individuals and are not persuaded by the PAC argument that giving is more effective if many small sums are pooled in a directed effort. They do not want to give to a committee that then decides on their behalf which candidates will be given support. They want to retain control and have the final say about who gets their money. (Permitting earmarking or paying real attention to recommendations may be essential to attract support from such individuals.) Political choices may be seen as a matter for individual judgment, as an area of privacy. Persons who hold this view are really questioning the legitimacy of the PAC idea.

The negative sell in which PACs may engage, to take account of the legal requirement to avoid coercion, may convince solicitees that they do not need to give, just as the assurance that anonymity will be protected can become a reason for nongiving. Among lower management, negative attitudes to senior management can be operating. In one instance the prominence of senior managers on the committee seemed to lead to the belief that they dominated the PAC. In another, PAC service by the CEO, who was known to be active in one of the political parties, seemed to turn off some lower managers, who drew the inference that the PAC would favor the CEO's party. One PAC officer observed that younger managers who were "children of the 1960s" tended not to give because of antiestablishment attitudes. They had not spent the years with the company that produced strong loyalties and personal identification. At the simplest level, noncontributors may be feeling financial pressures and assign the first priority on their income to personal responsibilities.

PAC officers adjust in various ways to the high nonresponse rates. Some are philosophical, others optimistic about the future, and a few frankly express disappointment. Some point out that it is necessary to have realistic expectations about how many eligibles will give; they feel their PAC is not doing badly. A few express suspicion when they hear of PACs with high response rates. They wonder how it is being done. Some are encouraged by improvement in the trend of giving. There is a general belief that the large numbers of nongivers is a challenge to improve the effectiveness of public-affairs programs.

In larger terms there may be some comfort to be derived from the high nonresponse rates. They are one of the surest signs available that the election law's requirements about avoidance of coercion are being respected by PACs. Also, the apathetics and cynics among nonrespondents seem very much like typical American citizens in their attitudes to politics. Finally, one is moved to inquire whatever happened to William Whyte's organization man. The junior executives among the nonrespondents are certainly not the group-minded, acquiescent conformists that Whyte envisioned as the emerging dominant type in America's executive suites.[12]

Summary and Observations

Money is the root of all corporate PAC activities. Without it there can be no effective implementation of campaign-contribution strategies. For PACs seeking to accelerate the increase of annual incomes, it is necessary to intensify fund-raising efforts end to expand their solicitation universes. There are obstacles, however, impeding full implementation of either course of action.

It does not seem likely that PACs will escalate solicitation to stockholders markedly in the future, even though organizations like the Chamber of Commerce have urged them to do so. Top management reluctance to approve solicitation of stockholders casts an equivocal light on the proposition that stockholders are the natural constituency of the corporation. The numbers and diversity of stockholders, the short-run nature of their concerns, and their unpredictable political preferences render it problematic that they can be rallied as a major source of PAC funding. Similarly, corporate-PAC policymakers discount the idea that use of the twice-yearly option might provide an additional supportive constiutuency. The corporate-PAC movement, reflecting as it does a business ethos, carries little appeal for blue-collar workers; moreover, their solicitation could trigger retaliation by union PACs.

PAC officers are aware that much work remains to be done to improve effectiveness of fund-raising procedures even in the case of presumably pro-business exempts, the great majority of whom have as yet to contribute to their company PACs; and it is on this constituency that most PACS must base their future expectations.

Corporate officers at the top level are an exception to the prevalence of high nonresponse rates. It appears, therefore, that if corporate PACs are to experience, in the early 1980s, a rapid rise in aggregate incomes by means of internal growth they must solidify at the lower levels of managment the kind of support that they obtain at the top echelon. Many are taking steps in this direction. Over 70 percent use or are going to use payroll deduction, which does stimulate giving. Thirty-one percent of Category B and 23 percent of Category C PACs that solicit only by mail plan to switch to a more personal approach. Presumably, others will follow and most will benefit from the change, although mail solicitation is likely to remain the exclusive reliance of those PACs whose constitutents number in the thousands.

Despite the desire to run successful PACs, management concern with employee morale, legal ramifications, public opinion, and possible negative congressional reaction tempers and restrains the urge to raise as much money as possible and contributes to imperfect mobilization. Consequently, most content themselves with one fundraiser a year, even though the law does not limit the number of annual solicitations; most avoid downhill solicitation, which is also permissible; few make any effort to enforce their guidelines for giving which, as a result, are seldom observed; and, in spite of the fact that the law does not require it, most have adopted stringent measures to safeguard the anonymity of respondents and nonrespondents alike. With few exceptions, it would seem that the PACS that have raised the most money have succeeded not because of coercive pressure but because they either already had politically active and concerned constituents or because their public-affairs programs have awakened formerly apathetic and skeptical nonrespondents to the idea that participation in the company PAC is in their interest as well as the company's.

Although solicitation of greater numbers of exempts, adoption of more personal approaches to fundraising, strengthened political-education programs, and increased expertise that comes from experience will undoubtedly improve response rates and yields, the indications from the data do not support the view that corporate PACs are poised to reap huge windfall profits by means of enlarged solicitation universes and intensified solicitation procedures. It is probable, therefore, that Clark MacGregor's hunch that half of the possible iceberg (measured in terms of internal growth) is already above water will prove close to the mark.

4 Organization and Administration

There is a sharp division, in the literature, in perceptions of the character of corporate PACs as organizations, and, in particular, of their relationships to their sponsoring corporations and top managements. Those who view them as legitimate expressions of the sectional interest of business, and as appropriate vehicles for the exercise of political voice by managers, are likely to stress the importance of the contributor constituencies in their affairs and their relative independence from the corporation and its leadership. One such friendly observer, for example, insists that the corporation's role in respect to the PAC is limited to decisions to sponsor it and to pay its administrative expenses and solicitation costs. In all other respects, it is asserted, "The corporation and the PAC go their separate ways." Top management has little to say about decisions concerning which candidates to support; members of committees that run PACs come from the executive ranks but "in the great majority of cases" have no direct relationship with the CEO.[1]

In a similar view, other sympathetic observers emphasize that PACs are "basically representative institutions that rely on a special constituency for support." Their essential feature as organizations is that they are completely dependent upon the support of voluntary contributors who have real power of choice whether to enter or leave the organization and ultimate influence over what the committees do with their money.[2]

In a more hortatory style, a prominent supporter of PACs expresses the expectation that committees will "not be a reflection of management prejudice. They should be fully democratic of purpose and fully democratic of decision, dedicated to issues of mutual interest and consequently supportive of mutually approved candidates."[3]

On the other hand, those who have been alarmed at the corporate-PAC phenomenon and see in it a new kind of threat of business dominance of the political process tend to portray corporate PACs organizationally as mere extensions of their sponsors and instruments of the will of top managements. The money that such PACs collect is considered only technically not the corporation's money. Management raises the money from "captive" employees, and management spends it. Corporations and their PACs are coterminous. For all practical purposes they are indistinguishable from one another. Corporate-PAC donations are "in truth and in fact" donations of the corporations themselves or at least constitute "back-door corporate financing of candidates." This is so because employees do not make contributions voluntarily but out of "fear of disfavor" or "hope of gaining in employer favor."[4]

This chapter represents an effort to bring empirical knowledge to bear on the controversy about the organizational character of corporate PACs and their relationship to corporate leadership. It examines the genesis of PACs, the composition of the committees that run the organizations, and their decision making. It then explores the extent of participation and influence of CEOs and of contibutor constituencies in the affairs of PACs.

The Genesis of Corporate PACs

Pre-PAC Political Contribution Programs

Only two of the seventy-one companies in the sample had PACs that antedate the 1970s. Nearly half (48 percent), however, reported that they had employee political contribution programs dating back more than a quarter of a century. There were two general types of program in the pre-PAC era: trustee plans and a pass-through or conduit system. Money-raising activities were confined in both, largely to the highest management stratum.

In the trustee plan, the corporation paid the cost of establishing and administering separate bank accounts for any executives wishing to participate. Because the law prohibited direct corporate contributions in federal campaigns, disbursement from the accounts would be made by a corporate official according to the preferences of the individual account holders. Although participants made their campaign contribution decisions individually, the trustee plan was in some respects a prototype for the corporate PAC. For example, a payroll deduction option was available to would-be contributors. A few corporations in the sample continue to maintain their original trustee plans, which were given formal legal recognition in the 1970s.[5]

Sixty-eight percent of those reporting that they had pre-PAC contribution programs utilized the more informal pass-through approach. Here contributions solicited from executives by a corporate official were funneled through the company to candidates. There were commonly used solicitation practices that many PACs would not today emulate—out of concern for legal considerations, employee morale, public relations, or possible negative government reaction. The CEO might undertake the solicitation himself, or might assign officers (called headhunters in one case) to conduct the "give-me-fifty-dollars" campaign. Usually, however, solicitation was the responsibility of the Washington lobbyist or a government-relations officer who would keep in touch with the company's senior executives through the year, pointing out to them those candidates that were good for the company. Once a year he would submit a list of recommended names and ask for money. In order to augment the impact of individual contributions, the double-envelope technique might be used. Here several individual contributions were delivered to the candidate in a single outer envelope with the company's return address stamped on it. Solicitors provided guidelines for specific amounts expected from contributors, usually based on a percentage of salary. Follow-up telephone calls might be made to those who had not given, to urge them to reconsider. Solicitation, conducted on a one-on-one basis, involved people who knew each other. There was no opportunity to depersonalize, through a neutralizing medium such as a committee, the emotional issues that come up dealing with political personalities. The pass-through approach, because of many unresolved ambiguities about what corporations were permitted to do, lay under a legal fog, that moved one PAC officer to recall that he had urged his CEO to drop it, lest it lead to jail sentences.

Experience with pre-PAC political contribution programs correlates significantly with the fund-raising success of corporate PACs. Fifty-seven percent of the sampled corporations that had earlier contribution programs appear among the top 100 PACs by total expenditures. By contrast, only 37 percent of the corporations that made no mention of pre-PAC operations have PACs in the top 100. PACs whose companies formerly had sponsored trustee plans are especially successful. Ninety percent of them are found in the upper two-thirds of the top 100 list of PACs by total expenditures. The more successful PACs have tended to be the ones that could clearly build on a considerable background of past practice. The corporations with such backgrounds were the earliest to take advantage of the new campaign finance legislation and to move to what is seen as the more effective PAC approach. In some instances, upper management personnel, who were already giving, welcomed the establishment of PACs as a relief from a lonely burden. Pre-PAC programs, by familiarizing company executives with the concept of organized political giving, helped lay the foundation for more effective PACs.

Establishing a PAC: The Timing of the Decision

The initiative in the establishment of PACs for two out of three of the companies in the sample came from Washington offices or public-affairs departments. Top management, particularly politically active CEOs, were the catalysts for the remainder.

In order for the PAC to be organized, the CEO (and occasionally the board of directors) has to give approval. In some instances, those urging a PAC had little trouble convincing their CEOs that a PAC would be in the best interest of the company. More often than not, however, proponents encountered caution and apprehension among top decision makers so pervasive that only ten of the seventy-one companies in the sample had formed PACs before 1976. Moreover, eight of these pioneer PACs were initiated in companies with previous experience of employee political contribution programs, evidence that familiarity bred acceptance.

For a number of reasons, most companies hesitated to follow the lead of the pioneers. In the first place, the corporate-PAC device was new, a product (with two exceptions) of the 1970s, and, thus, still in an embryonic stage. Company leaders considering the question of a PAC were dealing with an unknown quantity, one, moreover, that contained the potential for problems. This consideration suggested restraint rather than risk taking. Even to companies most interested in establishing a PAC, a wait-and-see policy seemed to make sense. Other companies had already formed PACs, and their experience could furnish a growing body of knowledge that the hesitant could utilize. Those that preferred to remain on the sidelines could chart the course of the more venturesome, study their organizational and procedural models, confer with them, and thus benefit from the experience of the pioneer PACs.

Above all, what held most companies back were uncertainties about the legality of the corporate-PAC device. Therefore, when the FEC in its 1975 Sun-PAC opinion, the Supreme Court in *Buckley* v. *Valeo* (1976), and Congress in its 1976 amendments to the Campaign Finance Act clarified the legal status of corporate PACs, the holdouts shed their remaining inhibitions and authorized the formation of PACs. As one interviewee described it, once the *Buckley* v. *Valeo* decision was handed down, "we took off." Four others specified the Sun-PAC opinion as the catalyst for their companies' decisions. Indeed, a public-affairs officer of one company used the Sun-PAC opinion to sell the idea of a PAC by arguing that it "was a way of correcting the abuses of Watergate, because it encourages small contributions." For the forty-eight companies that formed PACs in 1976 the move won general acceptance only after it became unequivocally clear that the device was legal.

For the remaining thirteen, however, CEO concerns persisted leading to delays of an additional year or more in the authorization of PACs. Still hesitant, top managements worried that overzealous solicitation might trigger negative employee reactions or lawsuits. They required more assurance that PACs would be purely voluntary and raise funds without any suggestion of coercion. Such CEOs were also affected by the climate stemming from Watergate revelations and allegations of corporate irregularities in campaign-finance contributions. Public-affairs officers who supported the formation of PACs had to dispel apprehensions that PACs could spark associations with Watergate and incite unfavorable reactions from employees, the public, Congress, and the courts. When these CEOs finally authorized action after 1976, they relied heavily on the advice of corporate counsel, tended to surround PAC operations with legal cautions, and assigned legal personnel a prominent role in the actual running of the PACs. They view their PACs as still an experiment and have been slow to permit full implementation, especially in the area of solicitation.

Motivations for Establishing a PAC

PAC officers were asked to indicate what, in their view, was the dominant consideration influencing their corporation's decision to sponsor a PAC. The five motivations most frequently mentioned by respondents (in order of priority) are (1) management recognition of the significant impact of government on corporate operations; (2) acknowledgment of the need of the corporation's Washington representative for adequate income with which to respond to the escalating importunities of congressmen and senators; (3) enhancement of political participation opportunities for managerial employees as part of their civic responsibility; (4) pressures felt by CEOs to emulate the example of peers who are reporting a successful experience with PACs; and (5) development of an effective counterbalance to the political influence of adversary organizations, particularly unions.

1. Recognition of the central importance of the government-business relationship appears in a variety of ways in the responses of forty-one PAC spokesmen (58 percent of the sample). A prominent concern of many is the experience of a geometric progression of government regulation during the 1970s. PAC activity is viewed as one vehicle for helping to reverse the trend to such overregulation. A spirit of resentment of what is perceived as government insensitivity to legitimate business concerns provides the animating energy behind such PACs. The future of the free-enterprise system is militantly proclaimed to hang in the balance, and bringing about change in the governing atmosphere in Washington becomes the central PAC purpose.

For others also stressing the importance of the relationship with government, the motivation in PAC formation centers less on reducing total regulatory impact than, as noted elsewhere, on securing more favorable outcomes from such regulation through enhancing access to congressional influentials. For corporations doing a large part of their business with the federal government, PAC formation is candidly stated to be due in large part to dependence on government contracts.

2. For Washington lobbyists the problem of responding adequately to fund-raising invitations from politicians is a major concern. The number of Washington fund raisers (receptions and dinners for which a donation is expected) has risen sharply, and the minimum amount expected has also increased. (One observer calculates that as many as 350 fund raisers were held in Washington between June 1977 and October 1978.)[6] An adequate source of income is required for Washington representatives who desire to see and be seen at such affairs. The provision of support for their Washington representative is reported as the key motivator of PAC formation by eleven PAC officers (15 percent of the sample).

3. Some public-affairs officers see PAC activity as but one part of an ongoing communication effort within the corporation to encourage managerial employees to become informed and involved. They are actively engaged in programs seeking to sensitize managers to their civic responsibilities and to develop awareness of government as the most significant external force affecting the enterprise. Nine respondents (13 percent of the sample) indicate that political activation of managers lay behind the decision to form a PAC.

4. The establishment of six PACs (8 percent of the sample) can be attributed to a kind of bandwagon effect. Initial CEO reluctance was overcome as a result of frequent interaction with peers who reported favorable experiences with PACs. The CEO might absorb such peer influences while serving on Business Roundtable task forces or as director on other corporate boards.

5. Four respondents (6 percent of the sample) mention defensive rejoinder to an adversary organization as the prime motivation. They are particularly concerned with counteracting union political efforts, praised as models to emulate. The corporate PAC is seen as providing politicians with an alternative to money from labor, enabling business to compete on more equal terms with labor in the political arena.

By far the most significant finding that emerges from this examination of the key motivations for corporate decisions to establish PACs is the high frequency of mention by PAC officers of government involvement in corporate affairs. The evidence provides independent confirmation of the observation of other students that the more pervasive or intensive the impact of government decisions on a corporation's operations, the more likely it is to charter a PAC.[7]

The Non-PAC Phenomenon

Although much attention has been lavished on the seemingly feverish activity of major corporations in forming PACs in the later 1970s, what may be called the non-PAC phenomenon has generally been overlooked. Large enterprises, it would appear, are just as likely not to have a PAC as they are to have one. Of the 1,000 largest industrials and the 300 largest nonindustrials listed by *Fortune*, 368 had formed PACs as of late 1979. Seventy-two percent of the largest corporations, then, had not yet established PACs. Among the first *Fortune* 500 (industrials), 202 or just over 40 percent had formed PACs; among the second *Fortune* 500, only forty-two or under 10 percent had them. By another measure the non-PAC phenomenon could be deemed even more impressive: Only 22 percent of the 3,755 corporations with assets of $100 million or more had PACs active in the 1978 election.[8]

The non-PAC phenomenon, when it is noticed, does not seem to reassure those who are worried about what they consider a definite prospect for the acquisition of inordinate influence by PACs. The fact that so many corporate PACs have sprung up in so abbreviated a period of time, and that there are still so many corporations that have yet to form PACs, suggest to hostile critics that the potential for enormous growth in the numbers of corporate PACs in the relatively near future constitutes a very real threat. The assumption implicit in such alarm is that, inevitably, the same motivations that have prompted a vanguard of large corporations to form PACs will eventually become operative among their more laggard cohorts. Some reason to doubt this expectation is afforded by the most recent data on rate of PAC formation issued by the FEC. These figures show that, while the number of corporate PACs is continuing to grow, it is at a decreasing rate.[9]

Is it, in fact, only a matter of time before major corporations thus far without PACs will jump on the bandwagon? Or is it possible that the corporations that have not, by now, done this are unlikely to do so in large numbers in the future? Is it possible that they are acting on the basis of a settled conviction that it is better not to get involved in PAC activity?

In an earlier chapter, it was pointed out that PAC growth can take place through internal expansion (of the amounts raised for campaign giving) of PACs already in being or through proliferation of the numbers of corporations that elect to have PACs. Certain obstacles to internal growth were then identified and judged likely to persist. It seems useful now to summarize the main factors that contribute to corporate reluctance to form PACs, keeping in mind that whether such factors prove persistent will affect in significant degree whether the future massive proliferation of PACs that some observers expect will actually materialize.

A distinguished student of campaign finance has commented that "some companies think it prudent to keep out of politics, even nonpartisan activities."[10] This statement, made on the eve of legislative action by Congress that gave rise to the PAC movement, continues to be an accurate characterization of attitudes toward political action that may still be found in the corporate world. For some corporate leaderships prudence seems to dictate avoidance of PAC activity. They worry about the potential of PACs to generate or increase public fear and adverse reactions. Despite the clarification of the legal status of PACs by court decision and legislation, they remain acutely aware that corporate PACs have real problems in winning public acceptance. Much of the public is only dimly aware of the growth of PACs and how they work, but large segments view the role of money in politics with suspicion, as an inherently corrupting force in political life. Given the widespread inclination of Americans to view politics as a "dirty game" and politicians as crooked and for sale, it is not surprising that top executives in some corporations are uncertain of how much acceptance the PAC idea would have if broached even to their own managers from whom the money for the PAC would have to be raised. Corporate PACs, on the whole, have not had good press relations. Such attention as the media have given to PACs has been pervaded by the theme that money buys influence, that it demands and receives a return in favors and even votes. Top managers must know that even Congress, which in 1974 and 1976 explicitly sanctioned PACs, showed signs in 1979 of restiveness about them, uncertainty about whether PACs were good or bad, and a developing inclination to cut back their spending capabilities, at least in House races.

A spokesman for a major oil company that has chosen not to have a PAC has noted that, although PAC political contributions are specifically legal, the public tends to view them as contributions made by the corporation itself and "does not perceive the legality of them."[11] A CEO, highly involved with public policy issues that affect his company and business in general, is not at all convinced that the public will learn to accept business PACs. Organized giving through PACs, in his view, creates the impression that the candidates backed are too indebted to business. Although "the public has learned to tolerate labor's PACs," he has doubts whether "it will tolerate the same thing from business."[12] A primary reason why some corporate leaders have not seen fit to allow PACs is that they consider the legitimacy of PACs, aside from their legality, fragile and untested by the public, wide sections of the media, and even with the managerial strata on whose commitment to give voluntary support the viability of PACs has to be based.

It will be recalled that PAC officers, when asked to explain why there were such high rates of negative response by eligible exempts to solicitation appeals, reported that some executives had philosophical objections to having PACs at all. They did not consider it the proper business of the corporation to be a focus of campaign giving; this kind of activity ought to be reserved for the sphere of privacy of the individual. This is, of course, a questioning of the legitimacy of the PAC idea. It is possible that, in the case of corporations that have stayed away from PAC formation, objections of this kind may be present at the highest level of management. Both prudential considerations and philosophical qualms play their parts in persuading corporate leaders not to charter PACs. In these respects there is substance in the shrewd inference of one of the more astute observers of corporate PACs that some of the "most die-hard anti-PAC voices [may] be found in the board rooms of the companies which do not have PACs."[13]

Some corporations in the 1970s were seared by the experience of being accused and widely condemned (although never actually convicted) of making illegal political contributions at home and abroad. In the aftermath, this issue has remained a major concern; a post-Watergate syndrome has remained alive, and top managements in the companies affected have shied away from sanctioning active and visible political involvement. For such corporations, there is a strong inclination to avoid even the appearance that they are again buying friends in high places with political contributions.

Although no major enterprise can be indifferent any longer to the growth of federal regulation, there are still important distinctions to be made in the degree of impact that such federal activity has on specific firms and industries. Corporations that elect not to form PACs are generally not facing on a daily basis regulatory and legislative battles, the outcome of which can be of crucial significance for their operations, as is the case for those that have formed PACs. Life insurance and retailing, for example, where the focus of concern about regulation has been on state capitols, are industries that have shown a low incidence of PAC formation.[14] An officer of a retailing PAC observed that line officers in retailing could come all the way up to top levels "without any need to worry about government." Such businesses are not very active in lobbying at the federal level and often did not bother to have Washington offices, depending instead on trade associations that are relatively unsophisticated politically. At high executive levels political awareness might be missing, and government relations would not be seen as part of normal business activity. Despite a burgeoning federal impact, many senior executives did not believe that government has become a partner. There is still a strong feeling present that it will go away.

It has been noted that in the formation of PACs certain key motivators have usually been present and playing an important role. Many corporations of substantial size, despite the movement of the last decade to establish Washington offices, still show no intention of doing so. Without the Washington representative and his need to see and be seen at fund-raising functions, one of the more active PAC promoters is absent. As external-relations concerns of major corporations have grown in recent years, public-affairs and government-relations departments have emerged, but their standing in management hierarchies varies widely. In corporations where government relations has not achieved recognition as a major staff function, another source of impetus for PAC formation may have only modest influence on corporate decision making. The balance of internal influence among various departments within a corporation may be decisive in determining whether a corporate CEO sanctions a PAC. Where legal or accounting departments with major weight in the corporation see serious legal problems or pitfalls in the detailed reporting requirements, they may be in a position to frustrate government-relations officers who are pressing for a PAC. (The reluctance of legal officers about PACs, even when overcome, may be institutionalized in the lukewarmness of the solicitation procedures that are adopted.) In the decision to have a PAC, the presence of CEOs who are politically active often has critical importance. But highly developed political consciousness is not an invariable accompaniment of high corporate office. It is possible that political activism among top corporate executives is still more the exception than the rule. It is worth recalling that distrust of politics and distance from politicians has long been endemic in the business world.

Altogether, it appears that there is a variety of factors acting as effective inhibitors of the formation of corporate PACs, helping to explain why many large enterprises have preferred not to enlist in the PAC movement. Some of these factors may prove to be temporary in their effect. The cleanliness issue is likely to wear off in its effect on companies hurt in the 1970s. (Already one major oil company that for a time refused to have a PAC because of such unhappy experiences has been engaged in a vigorous debate about whether to change policy.) The emergence of more significant federal regulatory impacts on some firms and industries will stimulate some to form PACs. The influence of some companies' successes in PAC activity may help others to overcome reluctance to enter the field. But some of the factors enumerated are likely to persist in their influence. Different ones may be compelling for different companies. In cumulative effect, however, they constitute an important restraint in the corporate environment on indefinite PAC expansion (especially at escalating rates of increase) that some worried observers have expected. It is likely that many of the large enterprises that are strongly motivated to form PACs have already entered the field and that the non-PAC phenomenon will remain an essential part of the total picture. Imperfect mobilization may be operating as much in the formation of PACs as in the internal expansion of already established ones.

The Internal Dynamics of the Committees

Structure and Composition

The membership of a corporate PAC consists of the administrative and executive personnel and stockholders who have elected to contribute to the separate, segregated fund that has been set up by the sponsoring corporation as authorized by law. The fund is managed by a political committee appointed from among its contributors. Most PACs have a single, undifferentiated committee that decides when and how to solicit and also selects candidates for support. About 70 percent of the PACs in the sample manage their affairs in this fashion. Thirty percent of the total, however, have established more elaborate committee structures. They have, first, a parent committee charged with the overall direction of affairs. Such committees may be variously designated as the board, the coordinating council, the steering committee, or the executive committee. In addition, they have established separate committees assigned special functions. Where the PAC operates with such a differentiated committee structure, it is the usual practice to assign candidate selection to a separate group. Such candidate-selection committees may consist entirely of members of the parent committee, or they may be a mix of officers from the parent committee and executives who serve only on the subsidiary committee.

If one examines the composition of parent committees and candidate-selection committees, a number of functional groups in the executive population stand out as the most frequently drawn upon for service. These are (in no order of priority) (1) legal officers, (2) financial-accounting personnel, (3) chief-executive officers, (4) government-relations-public-affairs specialists (including Washington representatives), and (5) what will be designated here as nonspecialist amateurs.

1. Legal officers: In twenty-six PACs in the sample, the corporation's chief counsel or some lower-ranking legal officer is found on the committees. In a few instances legal officers may attend committee meetings as resource persons without taking membership on the committees. The law does not mandate the presence of legal officers, but they are included by a substantial number of PACs, in order to give advice on legal issues that may arise, particularly in the solicitation area. Legal officers may be placed on the committees by CEOs to act as watchdogs of the voluntary principle and to insure that there is no excess of zeal in recruiting contributors. Their influence is reported by some PAC officers, who chafe against the restrictions legal officers insist upon, to be exerted on the side of caution and conservatism in interpreting what the law permits. Legal officers have, for the most part, little to offer in candidate-selection decisions. But some exceptions occur, particularly in airline and railroad PACs. Here the legal officers, because of the nature of the regulatory environment prevailing in these industries, are heavily involved with the political sector and have the expertise to be active contributors to the candidate-selection process.

2. Financial-accounting personnel: The law requires every political committee to have a treasurer and a chairman. When there is a vacancy in either office, no contribution or expenditure may legally be made. To assure continuity in operations, committees may appoint an assistant treasurer and vice-chairman, with the understanding that each succeeds automatically if

the office of treasurer or chairman becomes vacant. The treasurer of the PAC signs the reports made to the FEC, and he has the responsibility for completeness and accuracy. He makes certain that the required filings with the FEC are made on time, keeps the books and records, and insures that no illegal contributions are received or expended. He knows the names of the contributors and how much they have contributed. Inevitably, financial-accounting personnel, including the treasurer of the corporation, are drawn on to staff the position. PAC treasurers recruited from finance and accounting are not likely to play much of a role in candidate selection. They are on the PAC to discharge technical, legally mandated duties. However, there are occasions when the treasurer of the PAC does not come from the firm's accounting-financial staff. The secretary of the corporation or public-affairs specialists may occupy the office. In such cases, the treasurer of the PAC may assume a role in PAC affairs that goes beyond the legally required technical reporting functions.

3. Chief-executive officers: In eleven of the PACs in the sample (16 percent of the total) CEOs serve as members or officers of the PAC. (In two additional PACs they make significant inputs into the candidate-selection process without membership on the committees.) In seven of the eleven cases where the top corporate officers serve on the committees, it is worth noting that public-affairs officers are absent, suggesting that the CEO in the majority of the cases is accustomed to carrying on some of the more significant government-relations functions himself without delegating them to staff. (For more detailed discussion of the CEOs who serve on the committees, see the section in this chapter on CEO participation and influence in the affairs of the PAC.)

4. Public-affairs officers: Twenty-eight of sixty-eight PACs in the sample for which data are available (or 41 percent) do not have public-affairs specialists (including Washington representatives) on their committees as members or officers. In seven of the twenty-eight PACs, however, a public-affairs officer, even without membership on the committees, is actively serving as the chief source of recommendations in the candidate-selection process. In the remaining forty PACs, at least one public-affairs executive serves on the committees either as member or officer. In thirty-one PACs in this group, such executives are officers of the committees, as follows: Twenty-two (usually a vice-president of public affairs or a manager of government relations) are chairman of the PAC itself or of its contribution-selection committee; four are vice-chairmen of the PAC; and the remaining five serve as treasurer or secretary (or both) of the PAC. In nine, the public-affairs executive sits as a nonofficer member of the committee. (In eight of the forty there is more than one public-affairs executive on the committees, and in five of these eight there are enough of them to predominate numerically, especially on the candidate-selection committees.)

As the evidence abundantly illustrates, public-affairs officers constitute the most important single specialist group that participates in the running of the PACs. Vice-presidents of public affairs are the executives most frequently appointed as PAC chairmen. With the emergence of corporate PACs in significant numbers, assuming responsibility for the management of PAC affairs has become an additional important function of public-affairs departments. It will be recalled that in two-thirds of the PACs in the sample, public-affairs officers were the prime movers in generating the PAC. It happened usually because such officers took the lead in recommending the formation of a PAC to top management.

Such officers may spend only a fraction of their total company time on PAC activity. Nevertheless, their contribution is likely to be indispensable. They are the corporation's specialists in political affairs. Managing the corporation's relations with government and the political sector falls within their purview. They are the key group of corporate executives whose daily activity involves continuing contact with the political process. Their ascendancy in the affairs of the PACs results from this cardinal fact. Others on the committees are likely to have to lean heavily on their expertise and to be willing to defer to their judgment. They are employed, so to speak, to think and act politically on behalf of the corporation. They usually constitute the corporation's major internal resource and pool of professional knowledge about politics and government at both state and federal levels. They set the agenda, provide the briefings, and, in major degree, the recommendations on the basis of which candidate-selection committees make their decisions. They may be described as the staff, the administration, or the permanent bureaucracy of the PAC. They are appointed to the PAC by the CEO and are his main communication link to the PAC. Beyond their political knowledge, their influence results from the fact that the CEO may have delegated to them, contingent on the retention of his confidence and the setting of appropriate policy guidelines, the responsibility for effective conduct of PAC affairs.

The public-affairs officers who serve the PACs come from a variety of occupational backgrounds within the enterprises but, in a significant and growing number of instances, including some of the more effective PACs, they are being recruited by the CEO directly out of the political world. Former congressmen, unsuccessful House candidates, former governors, former White House staff, and former members of the staff of presidential candidates are among those now serving as PAC officers. Given the strategic role of such officers in PAC affairs, their political orientations are important and can influence the direction of PAC giving. A few are Democrats; many more come from the Republican ranks. Among the latter, one finds a mix of militant espousers of conservative, free-enterprise ideology and adherents of a moderate distrust of political dogmatism of either Left or Right.

5. Nonspecialist amateurs: This category consists of the largest number of executives who take service on the committees. Officers of thirty-one PACs (44 percent of the sample) state that one major consideration in deciding upon the composition of the committees is the achievement of representativeness and balance. Representativeness may mean a variety of things including: selection of executives from each of the major operating groups of the firm as well as corporate headquarters; choice of a cross-section of the corporation's operating and staff executive personnel; reflection of the various levels of the executive population solicited by the PAC; or a sampling of the geographical diversity and variety of plant locations of the firm.

The executives who are chosen for purposes of representativeness come from varied occupational backgrounds. They may be recruited from the range of professions and functional fields of management that are found in the contributor constituency of the PAC. They are even more distinctly part timers in their service to the PAC than are the public-affairs officers. More important, their service on the PAC is peripheral or perhaps entirely un-related to their ordinary round of executive duties. The time they give to the PAC is time spent on activity that takes them away from their regular work. Unlike the public-affairs personnel on the PAC, their work for the corpora-tion ordinarily does not prepare them directly for their duties as committee members or officers. For this reason they are designated as nonspecialist amateurs. Their civic activities outside of work, including volunteer activity in politics, provide them with the political background and knowledge they bring to their committee service. They may be chosen to serve because they have prestige and their names are recognized by other PAC contributors, or because they are known to have a record of civic service or participation, or have given some evidence of political acumen, activism, or interest beyond the ordinary. Appointed usually by the CEO, they are often the nominees of the public-affairs specialists. What they bring to the committees potentially is an ability to reflect the political outlook and sentiments of the contributor constituency from which they are drawn.

Committee Candidate-Selection Decisions

Are committee decisions about candidate support the product of real deliberation, with committee members in a position to make important in-puts and to exercise independent judgment? Or are the committees largely led or guided by one or a few specialists to whose judgment it is customary to defer? Are committee decisions genuinely collegial or are they ad-ministered?

In examining the nature of committee decision making, it will be useful to distinguish four types of committee situations, one or another of which will be found operating for almost all Pacs: (1) where the CEO serves on the committee; (2) where public-affairs officers are the major group on the committee; (3) where nonspecialist amateurs predominate numerically, and no public-affairs officers are visible on the committee or are otherwise serving as staff; or (4) where the committee consists of a mix of nonspecialist amateurs and public-affairs specialists, or where the latter provide the former with briefings and recommendations on candidates without being voting members of the committees.

1. The CEOs who serve on candidate-selection committees in the main participate actively in decision making, but in only a minority of such instances do they appear to dominate the proceedings. CEO presence does not automatically and inevitably prove incompatible with collegiality in committee decision making. Whether it is so or not may depend on the degree of CEO political knowledge and interest, and especially on the style of operation. As illustration, a case may be cited where the CEO was so inclined to avoid even the appearance of imposing his views and foreclosing discussion that he refrained as PAC chairman from casting the deciding vote, when the committee was deadlocked, about which candidate to support in a Senate race of special significance for the corporation and its executives.

2. Where a public-affairs group constitutes the core of the committee, it tends to be small (no more than three or four persons), meetings are informal, much of the decision making is by consensus (dispensing with formal votes), relatively easily arrived at by individuals who are in close communication.

3. There are a certain number of PACs in the sample (as many as 20 percent of the total) where the nonspecialist amateurs are alone on the committee without the visible presence or influence of public-affairs officers or of CEOs. These committees show signs of being genuine deliberative bodies. They hold formal meetings, engage in heated discussions, and really disagree on specific decisions. A precondition for the genuine collegiality that prevails is that the contributor constituencies involved contain many politically activated executives from whom it is possible to recruit lively and enthusiastic committee members.

4. The most prevalent committee situation by far is the one in which the committee consists of a mix of nonspecialist amateurs and public-affairs specialists or where the latter, without actual membership, provide briefings and candidate recommendations. By rough estimate derived from the perceptions of PAC officers who were interviewed, it appears that in about three out of five cases the specialists are the major influence or the dominant factor in candidate selection. Typically, in this kind of situation the public-affairs officers are described as submitting a list of candidates with reasons for their recommendations. They will be the only ones who provide such a list. Although the committee has the final say and may require good justifications, it will rarely reject, or even alter, recommendations.

Some PAC officers deplore rubber-stamp committees and express disappointment that their committees are not more participative. They have promoted two kinds of efforts to effect change. One way is to displace the original group of nonspecialist amateurs as too acquiescent and passive and to replace them with executives who, it is hoped, will prove more politically aware and knowing. It is too soon to say whether this kind of change has actually promoted more vigorous and assertive committees.

The other method has been to displace the public-affairs officers from the committees. However, change of this kind can be more cosmetic than real. If the specialists continue to be the mainstay and reliance of the committees in recommending candidates, their influence remains unabated even if they cease formally to be committee members. There are also cases where de facto recognition of the actual influence of the specialists has led to a different approach to reconstituting the committee: The nonspecialist amateurs have been taken off the committee and replaced by public-affairs officers, resulting in an entirely professionally run committee. Instead of trying to change the fact of specialist dominance, it has been thought better to acknowledge and further institutionalize its reality.

To put the matter in balance, it is necessary to take note that the mix of specialists and nonspecialist amateurs does not invariably result in the dominance of the former and the reduction of the latter to rubber-stamp status. Some mixed PACs report that they have meetings where the committee is split down the middle, where the nonspecialists produce their own recommendations, where acrimonious discussion occurs, and where the nonspecialists include independent thinkers.

A number of factors influence whether collegiality or rubber stamp results from the marriage of specialists and nonspecialists on the same committee. For example, PACs seem to differ in their ability to recruit nonspecialists who have enough real commitment to their committee activity to learn to hold their own with the specialists. It helps the nonspecialists to be more assertive if they can bring to the committee a considerable background of knowledge about local and regional political situations in the districts and states where their plants are located. Much may depend on the degree of interest of specialist officers in fostering a participative committee. Some may regard the selection of candidates as a task for professionals and so not view the passivity of nonspecialists on their committees as a problem.

CEO Participation and Influence

In the literature on corporate PACs, little has been said thus far about the nature of the influence and the degree of participation in PAC affairs by top corporate officers. In the main, stress has been placed on CEO remoteness from the PACs in their corporations, and their role has tended to be minimized. One source, for example, insists that CEOs hardly ever serve as PAC officers. Another asserts that most PACs have learned "to keep a considerable distance between themselves and top management of the sponsoring company" and that the committees "normally select their own chairman." The CEO's PAC activity is extremely limited.[15] Other observations, however, point in a different direction. One report declares that "the corporation has full authority and control over the structure of and appointments to the PAC" and that the most successful PACs have the "full backing and involvement" of top corporate officers.[16]

In the interest of contributing to more precise definition of the role of the CEO, it will be useful to specify the potential areas of CEO involvement as a preliminary to examination of the kind and amount of influence and participation that appears in the PACs in the sample. An accurate estimate of corporate leadership's PAC involvement requires assessment of how active CEOs are in respect to: (1) initiation and establishment of the PAC; (2) determination of the composition of the committee; (3) determination of the scope and methods of PAC solicitation; (4) participation in the solicitation process; (5) selection of the members and officers of the committee; (6) service as members or officers of the committee and degree of influence and participation in candidate-selection decisions.

1. Initiation and authorization of the PAC: The evidence shows conclusively the decisive contribution of chief executives in the genesis of corporate PACs. As has been previously noted, in a third of the PACs surveyed the CEO was either himself the prime mover or was so in combination with others. In all instances, whether he took the initiative or not, his authorization was required. In most cases before launching the PAC, the CEO will have consulted with relevant staff officers (public affairs, legal, personnel, accounting) and top-line officers as well. He will have determined, furthermore, whether or not to ventilate the issue before the board of directors and receive its sanction. Without the consent of the chief executive, whether given with enthusiasm or reluctance, there would be no PAC. Authorization means more, it should be understood, than merely the decision to have a PAC. It is the point at which the CEO has a major opportunity, by specifying conditions and guidelines, to shape the kind of PAC he wants to see emerge.

2. Determination of the composition of the committee: By composition is meant what might be called functional representation on the committee. Here the CEO's intervention is sporadic, but he may wish to insure that particular departments are strongly enough represented on the committee. For CEOs who are concerned about avoiding possible legal entanglements in reporting requirements or statutory stipulations against coercion in solicitation, it may be reassuring to have the corporation's legal department prom-

inently placed on the committee. One CEO with reservations about authorizing a PAC made a point of putting on the committee two corporate officers (the vice-president for personnel and the general counsel) who had voiced doubts about having a PAC at all in the consultations preceding the CEO's decision. The CEO might also intervene because he does not want the committee to be dominated by specialists. He may wish to minimize the role of the Washington office, or he may want to insure that headquarters' public-affairs officers are not too prominent. He may want the committee to give major representation to the nonspecialist amateurs who are the body of the contributors. In one case, the chief executive personally chose the committee with the intent of excluding all public-affairs personnel. CEOs, in summary, may interest themselves in the composition of the committee because they have some special convictions about what the appropriate mix in representation ought to be.

3. Determination of the scope and methods of PAC solicitation: CEOs have major inputs to make in relation to PAC decisions about whom and how to solicit. At the time of the authorization of the PAC, the chief executive may give careful consideration to how extensive a group of executives it is advisable to solicit. In a typical case, the CEO specified that solicitation was not to extend below the upper level of executives. Where the PAC has been operating on the basis of one solicitation universe and would like to alter it significantly, approval of the CEO is likely to be sought. In one company, PAC officers sought permission to enlarge the group of executives to be solicited, but the CEO resisted.

The law permits corporate PACs to solicit shareholders, but the decision to do so will not be taken by the PAC independently without authorization from top management. Such a step is seen as having too much potential impact on corporate-shareholder relations to be left entirely within the discretion of PAC officials. The relationship with stockholders, it should be remembered, is one to which CEOs give special attention. Up to this point relatively few PACs have solicited stockholders, despite the fact that some PAC officers show eagerness to do so. It may be assumed that top-management reluctance has been a primary factor in accounting for the sparse number of PAC efforts to reach out to this constituency. In a typical case the PAC chairman very much wished to initiate such solicitation, but top management was apprehensive and the matter continues under review.

In respect to solicitation methods, CEOs may set guidelines, when authorizing the PAC, that specify that a low-key approach to executive solicitees is to be utilized. They may require that solicitation of subordinates by direct superiors be avoided. The adoption of a payroll deduction plan will take place only after clearance from top management. More often than not, chief executive influence has been exerted as a brake on the enthusiasm of PAC officers for more intensive solicitation. But, on the other hand, some chief executives have encouraged more elaborate solicitation efforts in order to procure higher rates of participation. One CEO, disappointed with solicitation results, favored development of a slide presentation to supplement the usual letter. There have been others, furthermore, whose commitment to the success of the PAC leads them to countenance use of follow-up letters and downhill solicitations, among other forms of direct pressure.

In summary, the record shows that chief executive preferences are expressed and have weight in the area of solicitation policy. Where a significant change in scope or method is contemplated, the CEO will be consulted about proposed change. His consent will be sought, and it should be noted, will not automatically be given.

4. Participation in the solicitation process: PAC officers are often eager to enlist the services of the CEO as a resource to strengthen the solicitation effort. It is usual for CEOs, on authorizing the PAC, to write to the potential contributors announcing formation of the PAC, indicating his endorsement, and expressing the conviction that they ought to be participants. Some CEOs make speeches to at least the senior level of executives, urging them to become supporters. Most PACs solicit through letters; either the CEO or the chairman of the PAC will sign the letter. The CEO is likely to be the largest single contributor to the PAC. Solicitation material may, in fact, call attention to the sizable nature of that contribution and point out that the CEO is shouldering his obligation to the PAC in proportion to income. The implication is that others might consider doing likewise. Where the PAC has developed audio-visual presentations for solicitation purposes, it is usual for the CEO to appear and to endorse the PAC. In some cases the CEO shows reluctance to engage in direct selling of the PAC because of a wish to avoid any appearance of putting undue pressure on solicitees. They may prefer to stay strictly in the background. PAC officials in these cases may lament that the chief executive has not given the kind of active support needed to stimulate interest.

5. Selection of the committee: For forty of the PACs in the sample, adequate information is available relating to the process by which appointments are made to the committees that run the PAC. In thirty-one of these PACs, the CEO appoints all members, officers and nonofficers alike. In six the CEO makes some appointments, and the remainder are made by his appointees as follows: In two cases the CEO chose the PAC chairman, who then selected all the other members (the statement that the committees "normally select their own chairman" does not appear to be well-founded); or the CEO chose only officers who then proceeded to select the nonofficer members; or he picked the entire committee, whose chairman then selected the members of the candidate-selection subcommittee; or the entire committee selected by the CEO chose from its own membership the candidate-selection group; or he selected the chairman, with all other members chosen by lot from the PAC

contributors. In only three cases did the CEO appear to stand aside from the appointing process and leave it entirely to others: in one case to an executive vice-president; in another to an election by the fund contributors; and finally to the heads of operating divisions of the corporation. Top-side selection is overwhelmingly the rule. With but two exceptions, PAC contributors do not choose the committees that operate the PAC.

In making his appointments the CEO may lean heavily on the recommendations of others. Among those prominent in providing nominees are public-affairs officers, subsidiary presidents, or heads of operating divisions. Where the committee is large and seeks to include the variety of operations, geographical and functional, present in the company, as well as differing levels of the executive population, the chief executive cannot hope to have direct personal knowledge of the potential appointees and must rely on a screening process organized by others. However, there are surprisingly numerous instances in which the CEO is in a position to make selections from personal knowledge. This is likely to be the case when the committee is small and drawn largely from upper-executive levels at headquarters or the operating divisions. In all cases, it should be emphasized, the CEO is likely to have personal knowledge of at least one or two key appointees in whom he has confidence, who play highly significant roles in the running of the PAC, and who may function as his special communication link.

6. Service on the committee and contribution to candidate selection: In view of assertions that chief executives hardly ever sit on the committees or serve as officers, it comes as a surprise that corporate leaders are members of the committee in eleven of the PACs in the sample (16 percent of the total), and, in fact, are serving or have served as chairman of six of these PACs. The number is small, but it is certainly not negligible, and it raises questions about what prompts these CEOs to sit on the committees; how much influence they exert in committee on candidate selection; and whether there is any special relationship between their presence on the committee and the contribution strategy pursued by the PACs.

In eight of the subset of eleven where the CEO serves on the committee, a positive relationship with at least one of three factors was found to obtain: The CEO was the prime mover in formation of the PAC; or he had encouraged some form of organized campaign giving in the corporation in the pre-PAC period; or his background included a record of exceptional interest and involvement in politics. It may be inferred from such data that CEOs who elect to serve on the PAC have been accustomed to take a large and direct part in the government-relations activity of their firms and regard such activity as an essential component of their job.

It should be noted that all the chief executives in this subset serve on the special committee that makes candidate selections. In nine of the eleven cases, the CEO exerts an active influence on contribution decisions and in three of these that active influence amounts to dominance. (The number of CEOs with such active influence would increase to eleven if two others were included who, although not on the PAC, find opportunities to make significant inputs into the candidate-selection process.) Where the CEO chooses to take a place on the committee, it is clear that he does not stand aside from making his weight felt in candidate selections, although only in a minority of cases in the subset is he reported as dominating the proceedings.

Six of the PACs in the group of eleven were previously identified as pragmatic or pragmatic leaning in contribution orientation; four of them were ideological or ideological leaning; and one was indeterminate. Active participation by CEOs in PAC contribution decisions seems compatible with a variety of directions in contribution policy. The indications are that even if CEOs were to be an active influence on contribution decisions in most or all their PACs (they are not), there is not much likelihood that PAC contribution policy would proceed in a unilinear direction. Furthermore, the CEO who is active in contribution decisions does not appear to take the PAC, with very few exceptions, in a direction that differs from what one would expect, given the nature of the firm and the regulatory environment that it inhabits. The six pragmatic PACs in the group, for example, are either heavily regulated by industry-specific agencies (regulatory environment [1] as previously identified in chapter 2) or are engaged largely in businesses where the federal government is an important customer (regulatory environment [2]). The four ideological PACs in the group are all heavily impacted by the new regulation (regulatory environment [3]). With an occasional exceptional situation where the PAC is an extension of the personality and outlook of a dominant CEO-entrepreneur, CEO influence does not appear to be an independent variable that sets the PAC on a course that is different from what could be expected from the need to respond to the broad environmental factors impacting on the firm.

The discussion of CEO participation in contribution decisions has focused thus far on the minority who serve on the committees and are active in decision making. To put the matter in balance, it must be said that the great majority of CEOs stand aside from committee service and have a distinctly limited role in contribution decisions. Such CEOs may make occasional recommendations on behalf of specific candidates, and, as usually the largest single contributors to the PACs, their suggestions will be honored. They may have seen and approved bylaws adopted by the PAC and may have seized the occasion to make some input into the general statement setting forth the policies intended to guide the PAC in candidate selections. But individual decisions will be left to the committee overwhelmingly and to those whom the CEO may have appointed for their ability to provide special guidance in the making of such decisions.

PAC officers perceive the influence and degree of participation of chief executives in the PAC in various ways. Most see the CEO as relatively remote from the PAC and choosing to exercise limited influence. The CEO largely accepts direction from public-affairs officers, whose expertise is treated with respect. In this view the CEO seems to do little actively beyond insuring that he is kept informed. In only a minority of cases do PAC officers see the CEO as having a say in every phase of PAC activity.

Unless influence is distinguished from active participation, however, there is danger of unduly minimizing the role of the CEO. Two uniformities appear in the PAC involvement of CEOs that support their influence. They authorize the PAC, and, in so doing, specify conditions and guidelines that have large impact in shaping the PAC. They also exercise the power of appointment. The essence of their role here is not so much that they are in a position to choose the membership in its entirety, but that they can select the key personnel that serve the PAC and give it leadership and guidance. They are in communication with such personnel, and their relative distance from PAC operations rests on the confidence that the PAC has been entrusted to individuals who can be relied on to relate the activity of the PAC to the interests of the firm.

In addition, CEOs hold in reserve powers that amount to a potential veto on significant changes in policy or practice contemplated by PAC officials. Such departures will have to receive their assent. Most CEOs may prefer to remain in the background, but this should not be confused with absence of influence.

The Role of the Contributors

What the PAC spends in campaigns must be raised from the contributor constituency, although the expenses entailed in solicitation and otherwise administering the PAC are defrayed by the sponsoring corporation. This section seeks to shed light on the nature and degree of the contributors' influence and participation in the PAC. Earmarking and individual recommendations, two ways in which contributors have their say in PAC candidate selection, are given attention. The practice, widely condemned in PAC circles, of split giving is then examined with particular reference to its bearing on the relationship between committees and their contributors. The various approaches taken by PACs in fulfilling their widely acknowledged responsibility to report to their contributors on fund dispositions are described. The section concludes with an assessment of the contributor role in PAC activity.

Earmarking

Contributions to corporate PACs may be undesignated, leaving the choice of candidate to the committee. Contributions may also be earmarked. These are contributions designated for a specific candidate or organization (party or other) that are sent to the recipient with the PAC as intermediary. The PAC may pass on the contribution in the form of the contributor's check, or it may deposit the check to its own account and forward a new check to the candidate together with a letter of transmittal that identifies the contributor as a member of the PAC. A few PACs permit only limited designation. The contributor may choose a party or the upper or lower House to receive the contribution, but the choice of a specific candidate within these categories is left to the PAC. For purposes of contribution limits, earmarked contributions are attributed to the donor unless the PAC exercises some direction over the choice of the recipient.

Earmarking is not a highly regarded practice among experts who give advice to corporate PACs. They point out that contributions may be earmarked for candidates who might not meet the PAC's stated criteria, thus embarrassing the PAC or distorting the report of contributions that is available to the public through the FEC. If the PAC gives to one candidate and earmarked contributions are made to an opponent, the record will show contributions to both sides. The PAC may then be charged with opportunism. Earmarking also involves additional bookkeeping and reporting requirements.[17]

Despite such advice corporate PACs, in this as in most matters, tend to go their own way, and a considerable variety of practices results. Forty-three percent of the PACs in the sample prohibit earmarking. Twenty-six percent permit earmarking but note that the option is rarely exercised by contributors. However, another 31 percent allow earmarking and report that it occurs in significant degree, both in terms of numbers of contributors and amounts raised. From 5 percent to over 25 percent of total amounts raised are designated.

PAC officers are as divided in their opinions as in their practices on this matter. Those whose PACs do not permit earmarking, or those who regret having offered it in the first place, state firmly that it makes difficulties for PACs that seek to operate effectively and that it can defeat the purpose of the PAC. A PAC should be about pooling resources, they maintain, not conveying money on the basis of individual decisions. For maximum political efficacy, the money should be collected and expended in a directed, centralized way. PAC giving should carry the influence of many working together. A committee must have the flexibility to identify the most worthy candidates and make contributions that bear a determined relationship to need. Earmarked contributions may be directed to candidates who already have adequate funding or have no hope of being elected. Such earmarking is regarded as sheer waste.

A PAC needs to have and to follow a guiding philosophy of giving, and earmarking is regarded as incompatible with consistent application of that philosophy. It threatens constantly to disarrange the logic of the PAC. One officer noted that, when reporting to contributors about PAC decisions, he wanted to be able to explain why decisions were made and to show that dollars were spent in accordance with the way "we say we'll spend them." Even relatively small earmarked amounts can stand out in visible contradiction with the formal criteria established by the PAC. They may also give offense to other contributors. Earmarking can project a PAC into races where it might have preferred to stand aside or into races on the side of what it considers the wrong candidate. If the PAC supports one candidate in a race, an earmarked contribution inconveniently could appear on the other side.

The disadvantages of earmarking have led some committees that allow it to deemphasize and avoid encouraging its use. A few intend to discontinue the option after concluding that it is not in the interests of the company. One PAC has confined earmarking to choice of party or upper or lower House, after previously allowing designation of candidates. The latter practice was found to be an "horrendous administrative chore." But several PACs that allow it and express regret that they do still are not moving to give it up formally. Having once extended the option to contributors, they hesitate to withdraw it for fear that such action could be misunderstood.

If the case against earmarking seems so formidable, why, then, do we also find PACs, including some in the largest corporations, that seem relatively relaxed and comfortable about allowing it? For the 31 percent of the sample where earmarking is a live option, one answer is that it has proved appealing and preferable to more than a trifling number of contributors. In these PACs, earmarking increases the number of contributors and total amounts raised. Some contributors appear to want to give through the PAC and at the same time retain control of candidate choice. Earmarking can be a necessary condition for holding their allegiance. Some mileage for the PAC is obtained from these contributions, because they are conveyed in a letter of transmittal that notes that the individual making the donation is an employee of the company. These PACs do not seem to be very concerned about possible incompatibility between their guiding philosophy and earmarking. In their experience this problem has not materialized to a troubling degree. They seem to be willing also to bear the additional expense of processing fairly large numbers of earmarked contributions. One such corporation even bears the expense of allowing earmarkers to specify the precise timing of their contribution. Such PACs place major emphasis on stimulating civic involvement. If earmarking contributes to such results, they are all for it, and they will patiently process even miniscule contributions to (from one list) Common Cause (one dollar), Kennedy (five dollars), and Ribicoff (five dollars). The PAC officers see themselves as engaged in a long-term process of employee political-education and view PAC participation as one vehicle for such education.

In three cases information for PACs where significant earmarking takes place was sufficient to permit a more precise impression of what actually occurs. It is possible to compare, for example, designated and undesignated contributions in terms of party-support ratios and incumbency-support ratios. Observations can also be made on the frequency and circumstances in which two candidates were supported in the same race. The data are summarized as follows:

Company A: At least 25 percent of total contributions came from earmarking. There were 350 donor-identified contributions and 189 designated by committee. Seventy-five percent of total PAC-designated contributions in federal races went to Republican candidates; 85 percent of total earmarked contributions went to Republicans. Incumbency-support ratios were similar: 42 percent PAC-designated and 40 percent earmarked. There were no instances in which PAC-designated contributions or earmarking resulted in support of both candidates in any race at the general-election stage. Despite the considerable amount of earmarking, no split giving resulted.

Company B: Over 15 percent of total amounts contributed by the PAC at the federal level were contributor designated. Of PAC-designated contributions, 69 percent went to Republicans; of earmarked contributions, 92 percent went to Republicans. In four races the committee made contributions to both candidates; the FEC printout shows no instances in which earmarked contributions resulted in support of both candidates in a single race.

Company C: Again, over 15 percent of total amounts contributed were earmarked. Party-support ratios were similar: 73 percent of PAC-contributed funds and 76 percent of earmarked contributions went to Republicans. Fifty-nine percent of PAC-designated funds and 86 percent of earmarked funds went to incumbents. (This disparity is due to the rally of support by earmarkers around one Republican incumbent who was fighting for his political life.) No PAC-designated funds were expended to support candidates on both sides of any race in the general election. Forty-two earmarked contributions were made on behalf of one candidate in a single race, amounting to over $4,000; three PAC members designated a total of $100 to the other candidate in the same race. There were also two instances in which an earmarked contribution went to support the opponent of a PAC-funded candidate.

Three cases of significant earmarking are not sufficient to demonstrate anything conclusively, but they are surely interesting and suggestive in their possible implications. What deserves emphasis is that the overall directions of contributor-designated and PAC-designated giving run strongly parallel, indicating that it is possible to exaggerate how much danger there is that earmarking will disarrange the logic of the PAC. Individual designations may not seem to be readily compatible with centralization of PAC giving, but the contradictions in patterns of donation between individual choices and committee choices in the aggregate in these three cases are not that great. The indications are that it may not be sufficiently frequent to cause the PAC embarrassment at having to attach the company's name to a letter of transmittal of a member-designated contribution. This view is further supported by the data about split giving. Committee decisions were as likely to produce split support of candidates as was earmarking. It seems extreme to maintain that most split giving is the result of earmarking. (More conclusive data on this point are presented in the section on split giving.)

Committees and their constituencies do not appear to be widely out of touch with each other in their donation preferences. Where there are differences, they do not seem to be substantial with one important exception. The earmarked contributions show consistently higher Republican-support ratios than the committee-designated ones. The earmarkers appear to be more strongly partisan and more consistently ideological in their giving than are the committees. This is understandable since the PAC may be responding in its decisions to a wider range of considerations, including some quite pragmatic ones, than enter into the decisions of individuals. Some PAC managers who dislike earmarking criticize earmarkers for not adhering to basic PAC-contribution criteria, but it is equally true that earmarkers may feel that the committee itself does not adhere strictly enough to their own understanding of the contribution criteria. When asked whether their members had any complaints, PAC officers mentioned that contributors occasionally criticize the PAC's party-support ratio. This usually means that they would like to see it support more Republicans. It may be that such contributors find the earmarking option appealing. Apparently, earmarking can fulfill a kind of safety-valve function for the PAC in its relations with its constituency. It enables the PAC to hold the allegiance of members who might otherwise be disaffected because of their conviction that the committee is interpreting the contribution guidelines too pragmatically.

A large number of PAC officers view earmarking as an undesirable practice. At least fragmentary evidence, however, indicates that some of the harsh criticisms and dire expectations presumed to flow from it can be overdone. In particular, split giving appears to occur as frequently from committee decisions as individual ones. Earmarking can help to enlist contributors who want to retain control of their giving, and it can enable PACs to retain contributors who do not sympathize with the overall trend of their PAC's decisions.

Contributor Recommendations

An impressive percentage (at least 90 percent) of the PACs in the sample indicate that they seek recommendations from individual contributors. Many who do not allow earmarking view individual-contributor recommendations as the desirable alternative. Some indicate that such recommendations are rarely turned down. Others are more guarded. Their PAC literature states that recommendations will receive every consideration, but that decisions must ultimately rest with the committee, and that the committee reserves the right to reject recommendations that are not in harmony with the contribution criteria set forth in PAC bylaws. A few provide forms that require the contributor to supply data about the candidate proposed. Such forms, if too elaborate, can have a chilling effect, because they may amount to asking the PAC member to do considerable data collection that may be beyond his inclination or capabilities. A few PAC officers state forthrightly that recommendations are not sought nor expected; they explain that their contributors express confidence in the judgment of the committee and are content to have it exercise full discretion in the disposition of PAC funds. The contributors may even look to the committee's candidate-selection decisions for guidance in their own voting.

Less than 25 percent of the PAC officers who state that they welcome contributor recommendations express satisfaction with the actual flow of such recommendations, a clear indication that, in most cases, the volume is small. Those who are most successful in this regard have gone beyond formal statements that they will entertain recommendations and have taken active steps to encourage contributor initiatives. In their literature they stress their receptivity to recommendations and give directions about whom to contact and by what means. They promise that such recommendations will get most serious consideration, that they will be brought to the committee and acted upon, and that the contributor will be notified whether a recommendation has been accepted or turned down. If the suggestion is rejected, the committee will explain why. In a variety of ways such PACs have also developed organized networks away from corporate headquarters, at the operating levels of the corporation, to solicit and receive recommendations. They have set up subcommittees or advisory committees or plant coordinators who are on the spot and known to the contributors and who channel recommendations to the candidate-selection committee.

Contributor recommendations can raise problems in their own way as troublesome as those that earmarking creates. Some individual recommendations accepted by PACs have as little in common with the logic of the PAC's professed policies as earmarked choices. PACs may entertain and honor recommendations from high status individuals in the company who make large contributions, although the recommendations may be governed by personal, even idiosyncratic considerations. Or committees, because they want to encourage participation of contributors and to avoid offending them, honor recommendations that are not in harmony with contribution criteria, or that even result in support of both candidates in a single race.

Such PACs are willing to make these considerable concessions to show responsiveness to the expressed wishes of contributors. They are well aware of their dependence on voluntary contributions from constituents who can withdraw their support; they want to stimulate the feeling that contributors are an integral part of the organization and that, in a real sense, the PAC is providing them with an outlet for expression of their political preferences.

Split Giving

Split giving is the practice of contributing to more than one contestant in an election. It can take a number of forms. The PAC may contribute to the opponents in a general election; or it may contribute to one contestant in a primary and the opponent in the general election; or a contribution may be made to a victorious candidate soon after the general election, to help defray a deficit, after the other candidate had been supported and defeated. One PAC officer even extended the definition to include a case in which his committee, in 1976, supported a challenger in a close race and then, in 1978, supported the incumbent in a rematch of the same candidates. It should be noted that split giving can also mean that equal sums are given to both candidates.

Split giving is a sensitive area of contribution policy for many PAC officers. It is the object of adverse comment within PAC circles. An otherwise sympathetic observer of corporate-PAC behavior has noted with dismay that in 1976 there were "numerous cases" where contributions were made to both candidates in general-election contests.[18] Criticism of this kind seems to be having some effect; the data show that split giving was relatively rare in the election of 1978. If one considers that the corporate PACs in the sample made, in the aggregate, several thousand contribution decisions, the number of decisions involving split giving is very small. They amount to less than one such decision, on the average, per PAC or around 3 percent of the total number of decisions made by the PACs surveyed. This being so, one can legitimately inquire why any attention is paid to split giving. The answer is that such decisions, few as they are, repay study because of the light they shed on PAC motivations and attitudes and on the kinds of pressures within PAC environments that can lead to the practice.

Because of the moralistic flavor of most discussion of split giving, it might be well to state at the outset a key conclusion reached after examination of the data. It oversimplifies a fairly complex phenomenon to believe that the practice is the result of cynical, amoral political opportunism and uniformly reflects discredit upon PACs that engage in it. Split giving, like most seemingly contradictory kinds of behavior, tends to be a response to conflicting pressures, in this case generated by key political-contests that assume special importance for the committees and their constituencies.

Thirty-seven PACs, 52 percent of the sample, engaged in no split giving in 1978 general-election contests; thirty-four PACs, 48 percent of the total, engaged at least once in such split giving. Of these thirty-four PACs, nineteen engaged in the practice once (56 percent); nine engaged in it twice (26 percent); two engaged in it three times (6 percent); and four engaged in the practice four or more times (12 percent). Fifty-four percent of the ideological and ideological-leaning PACs and 48 percent of the pragmatic or pragmatic-leaning PACs did not engage in split giving in the 1978 general election, a discernible but not marked difference.

The FEC printouts for the seventy-one PACs surveyed show sixty-two cases of split giving in general-election contests. In fourteen of these, there are indications that earmarked contributions were made. In nine of the fourteen, although earmarking was present, the PAC itself contributed to both candidates. Earmarking, then, was the sole cause of split giving in under 10 percent of such cases.

A classification of PAC officers' attitudes to split giving is possible. The large group whose PACs have refrained from the practice wish to see it generally discountenanced. They are emphatic that this is not what PACs should be doing. They see it as designed to gain favor and as demonstrating a complete lack of integrity. Some also condemn it as a destructive political strategy, insisting that it forfeits the respect of the candidates. Among those who engaged in the practice in one general-election contest in 1978, moral disapproval tends also to run high. This group was divided in reactions to questions about the single case of split giving. Some found the experience distasteful, were reluctant to discuss it, and limited themselves to suggestions that it happened because of personal requests or unspecified special circumstances. Others (among the group who engaged once in the practice) discussed the considerations that entered into the decision in detail, so that the exceptional circumstances that prompted it could be clarified and the imputation of political opportunism could be removed or mitigated. Those who engaged in split giving in general-election contests two or more times tend not to see it as a moral issue. They are matter-of-fact and relaxed about it. Speaking from actual experience, they insist that candidates understand and do not despise PACs for it, because who better than politicians can understand actions prompted by political necessities. Among this group are PAC officers who do not see actions motivated by political opportunism as necessarily morally tainted. From their point of view, "this is the way the game is played."

Reluctance to talk about split giving may be prompted by guilt feelings in part, but it is also due to concern about the possibility that unsympathetic or uncomprehending reporting of it may cause embarrassment to the PAC and its parent corporation. An actual case is worth recounting, because it indicates that such concern is not unwarranted. A young reporter for a major newspaper in a state where a number of corporate PACs had recently sprung up was assigned to do a piece about the emerging PAC phenomenon. He did some telephone interviews and his homework at the FEC public-records office in Washington and found the PAC printout of one of the largest corporations in the state showing contributions to three candidates for the same office. The printed column duly reported the three contributions without any explanation of attendant circumstances. (One of the contributions, for example, was earmarked and given in a primary.) The PAC officer commented bitterly that the corporation, whether because of hostile or inexperienced reporting, was made "to look like a whore."

Although split giving tends to be under a moral cloud in general-election contests, this kind of giving in primaries is warmly approved. The form in which split giving occurs in primaries is usually in combination with giving in the general election. In a typical example, the PAC expecting to support a particular candidate in the general election, enters the other party's primary to support the likely rival, because it wants to help him defeat a totally unacceptable opponent in the primary. Even if the undesired opponent wins in the primary, the PAC will contribute to the candidate of the other party, whom it favored all along for the general election. Occasionally, a dilemma arises if the candidate that the PAC favored in the primary wins. Usually the PAC shifts its support to his rival in the general election, in these circumstances, but sometimes it may feel that it cannot, in good faith, desert the individual supported in the primary, and so split giving in the general election results. Most corporate PACs are not very prone, at least so far, to supporting candidates in primaries. For the PACs surveyed, there were eleven cases where one candidate was supported in the primary and where the opponent was then supported in the general election.

It remains to inquire about the motives that prompt contribution committees to give money to both candidates in general election campaigns. Examination of the decisions reveals that there are a limited number of typical situations that may be summarized as follows:

1. Here both the contribution committee and its constituency are divided about which candidate to support in a district or a state that has major economic significance for the corporation. Large numbers of employees at important company locations are found there. The race may have achieved national prominence, and interest in it runs high among PAC contributors.

Example: In a Senate race in a state where most of the PAC members are located, the contributors were recommending both candidates, and the committee itself was split down the middle. The candidates were invited to appear before the committee and present their views on business issues. The committee's opinion was that it had to tread carefully to avoid alienating many contributors. It decided to conduct a poll to elicit the preferences of the members of a company citizen-action committee in the state. A sum of money was set aside and divided according to support ratios in the poll.

Seventy percent went to one candidate and 30 percent to the other. The PAC officer explained that the split giving was done in the interests of preserving the vitality of the PAC.

2. The expressions of preference from PAC members are uniformly for one candidate; there is strong hostility to his opponent. The committee, however, is divided.

Example: In one district the incumbent was disliked by the industry and considerable sentiment for the challenger was being expressed at company sites. There was a sharp division in the committee. Some committee members supported the constituency-preferred candidate. Others urged that the incumbent was not easy to defeat, that he held the chairmanship of a key committee that dealt with important industry interests, and that he had not always proved unfriendly, that he could be talked to. The committee decision was to support both candidates, with the larger sum going to the incumbent. The point in giving a donation to the challenger was to send a message to the incumbent and let him know that he was not untouchable.

3. Again the trend of sentiment at the plant level in the district or state is heavily for one candidate. But the committee is united in the view that an important case for the other candidate is being overlooked by the contributors.

Example: There was much sympathy in the committee for the incumbent, who had strong support at plant sites as well, but the incumbent had been making a sloppy campaign. The outcome was in doubt. The race was in a crucial state for the corporation, which would need to look for important support in Washington from the winner. The committee decision was to give to both candidates, with the larger sum going to the incumbent. When the challenger won, an immediate additional donation was made to help with his deficit.

Example: The contributors and the committee were more sympathetic politically to the views of one candidate on general business issues. The incumbent was a committee chairman, a man of major influence in Congress. The committee felt that it could not avoid giving him money. Donations went to both.

4. The committee gives great weight to the preferences of its constituency in the district or state. But constituency sentiment runs high for both candidates.

Example: In a key race, contributor opinion, reflecting the closeness of the race, was almost evenly divided. The committee gave equal amounts to both candidates.

Example: In one state the corporation has two divisions. One division's managers favored one candidate because of stands of interest to a railroad. The second division favored the other candidate because of stands of interest to a mining concern. In a crossfire of divisional preferences, the PAC contributed to both candidates.

5. The committee has ties of loyalty and interest that attach it to both candidates. It finds a decision difficult to make because both candidates are acceptable and, indeed, well respected.

Example: Senior officials of the company knew the senator. When they went to him with a problem, he was thoughtful, alert, and incisive. He was consistently helpful. But the challenger was a congressman whom the company also knew. A third of the company employees in the state worked in his district. He was responsive, even if he did not always vote the way the company might have wished. The company was pleased to have dealings with him. The PAC manager's view was that it was necessary to "operate with some loyalty in the political world." The committee gave donations to both candidates, with much the larger amount going to the incumbent. An additional contribution was made quickly to the victorious challenger's "deficit party" after the election.

6. Committee preferences are clearly for one candidate. But it feels obliged to take account of representations on behalf of the other candidate from influentials within the company.

Example: The committee favored the challenger, but top executives who reside in his district knew the incumbent, considered that he listened well, and had background in the industry.

7. Some PACs embrace opportunism willingly. They frankly hedge. Some races are so important, because of company locations in the district, that they wish to be with the winner. There is no shame about it. It is necessary self interest. In this category belong PACs whose managers explain that late in the campaign they made a contribution to the rival of a contestant originally backed, because the rival then seemed likely to be the winner. Here also belong PACs that, having previously backed the wrong candidate, hasten to establish constructive relationships with the victor.

In a minority of cases, split giving occurs because of opportunistic considerations. The PAC managers are committed to maintaining open channels of communication with whomever wins. But overwhelmingly split giving happens in situations where the PAC encounters difficult conflicts. The PAC has to manage its relations with contributors effectively; it has to respond to pressures from influentials who cannot easily be ignored; conflicts within the committee have to be resolved; ties of loyalty may attach the PAC to both candidates; specific company interests may exert a pull toward one candidate at the same time that the PAC feels more affinity for the other candidate's views on general business issues.

One way to deal with such conflicts would be to contribute to neither candidate, and there are indications that PACs occasionally choose this alternative. One PAC reported to its contributors that there were several races in which both candidates were probusiness. The races were, therefore, avoided to forestall split giving. Since funds were limited it was considered better to spend them in races where there was a possibility that an antibusiness candidate could be defeated. In some key races, however, the PAC cannot choose the path of avoidance without a risk of forfeiting respect. To cite an example, it was simply not possible for PACs in the energy-resources field to look the other way in the Krueger-Tower Senate race in Texas even though the decision was a troubling one to many committees.

Split giving, it seems clear, is not going to disappear completely in the foreseeable future, despite the strong moral disapprobation it incurs in some PAC circles. For a minority of PAC officers, opportunism is seen as an essential feature of all politics; they do not view split giving as a subject for moral reproach. Even among those PAC officers and their committees most troubled by it, occasional cases of split giving are likely to continue to occur as one way of responding to cross pressures in key races.

Reporting to Constituents

The Federal Election Campaign Act requires corporate PACs to inform employees being solicited of the political purposes of the fund. In order to respond to this requirement, PACs uniformly have developed bylaws (usually distributed to the solicitees) that contain a statement of purpose and also set forth the criteria intended to serve as guidelines for candidate-contribution decisions. The law, however, does not require PACs to report to their contributors what has been done with the money raised, although, of course, it requires them to submit detailed reports to the FEC of amounts raised and expended.

Nevertheless, even in the absence of legal stipulations, PACs find it desirable and useful to periodically render to their constituency an account of contributions and expenditures. The PACs in the sample overwhelmingly engage in such reporting; there were only five instances (under 10 percent) in which such reporting was not done.

A variety of considerations enters into the decision to report: the data have already been compiled for FEC purposes and can easily be passed along to relevant employees; such reporting is seen as an essential element in effective communication between the committee and those who have elected to contribute and those who might elect to contribute in the future; the contributors are likely to have an expectation it would be perilous to disregard, that they will be informed by the PAC about what has been done with their money; reporting is a condition of maintaining interest and cementing loyalty; most important, reporting can be used to demonstrate that PACs have made effective decisions in keeping with bylaw guidelines. Reporting may also be synchronized with solicitation appeals, both to help persuade current contributors to continue their giving and to enlist new supporters.

Because the tendency to report is so widespread, special interest attaches to the governing reasons and attitudes in the exceptional instances of the five PACs that decline to do so. In one case of a closely held corporation whose PAC contributors consist entirely of large shareholders, informal communication was considered sufficient to make the contributors who might be interested aware of the details. Two PACs stated that they had lapsed from reporting because of inertia. After a few years of operation, both had slipped into a state of reduced activity, but there were ambitious plans for revival, and it was anticipated that there would be a resumption of reporting in the near future. Two other PACs had never seriously considered issuing reports. In the first case it was explained that the information was available and that interested persons could visit the secretary of the PAC and examine it. In the other case the PAC indicated a preference not to publicize information about its contributions on the ground that it did not want candidates to know what the PAC did in order to avoid candidate animosity. This position was adhered to despite the fact that the information was on file and accessible to the public at the FEC and despite awareness apparently that staff assistants of congressmen were not strangers to the public-records office of the FEC.

If the commitment to report to constituents is widely acknowledged, some important nuances of difference in PAC practice are observable in the characteristics of the actual reporting. Most PACs report once or twice a year. Their most elaborate report tends to be made soon after the November election every second year. This report will consolidate the data for an entire election-campaign cycle (the previous two years). More perfunctory reporting may be done of PAC off-year election activity, although the pace of activity in the off-years seems to be accelerating. A few PACs, especially those that have newsletters, may report on a quarterly basis; as quarterly data are compiled and sent to the FEC, a summary is conveyed, through the newsletter, to constituents.

It should be noted that two PACs indicated that they had received complaints or suggestions about the timing of reports. There was some unhappiness, reflecting quite different degrees of confidence in the respective PACs, that reporting had not taken place until after the November election. In one instance, members seemed to want more opportunity to guide the PAC. Their criticism was that the committee had not furnished interim reports prior to the election and that members, therefore, did not know what was being done with their dollars. In the other case, to the contrary, members wanted more opportunity to obtain guidance from the PAC. They urged some pre-November reporting, so that they would have the benefit of PAC advice in making their own voting decisions.

Some lack of uniformity appears in the definition of the group of employees to whom reports are sent. Some PAC officers emphasize that the reports were conveyed to all eligible employees solicited by the PAC, contributors and noncontributors alike. They were at pains to explain that it was desirable to report to all solicited employees to protect the anonymity of givers and nongivers. If this was done, furthermore, it was possible to combine the report with a solicitation appeal. But some PACs appear to send their reports to contributors only. Those that do may mail the report to the contributors' homes as a safeguard of anonymity.

Typically, PACs report aggregate amounts raised and expended and provide a list of candidates supported, with indications of whether they won or lost, party affiliation, and status as incumbent, challenger, or open-seat contestant. If they permit earmarking, designated and undesignated aggregate amounts may be noted; candidate selections resulting from earmarking will usually be indicated. In some instances, something less than full disclosure is made in the reports. A few PACs do not list the candidates, for example, providing only summaries of amounts raised and expended. Although the reason is not clear, the possibility exists that such PACs may not wish to open themselves to contributors' criticisms for some of the candidate-support decisions they have made.

The most significant area of divergence among PACs in reporting practice occurs in respect to the amount and kind of analysis and interpretation that accompany and give meaning to the quantitative data. Some PACs content themselves with reporting the data, leaving the figures to speak for themselves. This approach tends to appear among PACs run entirely by part timers who are busy with other duties over and beyond their PAC responsibilities. Their reporting may be dutiful but perfunctory. Or the data may be stated without amplifying explanation by PACs that are highly confident that they have the assured support and understanding of their purposes by contributors. A few PACs run by professionals are inclined to operate on the premise that they have discharged their obligation to contributors by stating the magnitudes and listing the candidates. They are self confident about their expertise in the disposition of PAC funds and little inclined to acknowledge a responsibility to defend and explain why and on whom they expended PAC money.

Through much of the reporting by PACs, however, there runs the conviction that it is not sufficient merely to report the facts, but that it is advisable to make the case to contributors that funds have been expended wisely and in consonance with stated PAC-criteria. In the selling of PACS to solicitees, there is frequent emphasis on PAC giving as preferable to individual giving, because resources are pooled; expert direction is provided; and a coherent strategy of giving can be applied; all tending to concentrate and maximize impact. Inevitably many PACs in reporting feel obliged to resell the PAC, that is, demonstrate that their record of giving substantiates the claims made on behalf of the superior results of organized giving. PAC officers will want to present to their constituency proofs, or at least strong indications, of the efficacy of their contribution strategy. The most frequent reliance by PACs in demonstrating such efficacy is the win rate. Over 25 percent of the PACs in the sample cite the high percentages of winning candidates supported or the high percentages of total amounts expended on behalf of winners. PAC bylaws often include, in their enumeration of contribution criteria, the expectation that candidates, to merit support, must be perceived as having a reasonably realistic chance to win their contests. It is emphasized that PACs are not in business to make philanthropic or quixotic gestures on behalf of hopeless causes. Too many losers on the PAC list might be viewed as a discouraging sign of PAC ineffectiveness. Money well spent seems to be money spent on winners.

Both pragmatic and ideological PACs in the sample call attention to their win rates in reporting, but there is a significant difference in emphasis. The pragmatic PAC is in a more advantageous position to rely heavily on win rates as the indicator of effectiveness. Given the electoral advantages that incumbents normally enjoy, the tendency of pragmatic PACs to support incumbents, not surprisingly, produces high win rates. Some PAC officers are suspected, in PAC circles, of supporting incumbents in great numbers in order to point to high win rates as evidence of their political acumen and effectiveness. The interview data include instances in which PAC officers admit that they support incumbents because they have to produce winners to hold contributors. But the major investment in incumbents by pragmatic PACs is not made cynically to exploit high win rates. It is, rather, an essential part of a contribution strategy related to developing and enhancing access to politicians in strategic congressional positions allowing particular influence on the outcome of issues pertinent to the parent corporation. Among pragmatic PACs there are cases of reporting that go beyond win rates to develop other kinds of evidence of effective PAC giving. One PAC, for example, reported with satisfaction that 80 percent of those receiving contributions were elected, but it also pointed to a legislative issue of special importance to its industry, where the House vote indicates 99 percent support from incumbents previously supported by the PAC. Here an effort was made to relate PAC giving to legislative results, not with an implication that the PAC's money bought votes, but that candidates likely to be supportive of company positions had been identified with great accuracy by PAC officers.

For proof of efficacy ideological PACs would be in an uncomfortable position if they tried to rely on win rates. They support relatively high percentages of challengers and open-seat contestants, and win rates, they understand and expect, will be adversely affected. Because they have more difficulty demonstrating that PAC money has been used fruitfully, ideological PACs more often than pragmatic PACs produce sophisticated analyses and interpretations of the purpose and results of their giving. In so doing, they contribute to deepening the political education of their constituents. A limited number of examples of the alternative approaches of the ideological PACs are worth citing as illustrations:

1. PAC I observed in its report that it had looked for and found a number of House and Senate probusiness incumbents. The win rates for these incumbents ran high. The PAC also supported a set of challengers to incumbents deemed hostile to business. Of sixteen such challengers, only four were elected. But contributors were urged to understand that it was absurd to overemphasize the win rate. The PAC's purpose was to help bring about a more responsible Congress, and this could be done only by replacing some incumbents and moderating the attitudes of others. The unique feature of PAC I's reporting was that it gave the percentages of the vote attained by the candidates on its list. These figures showed that eight of the twelve losing challengers had run close races and captured over 40 percent of the vote. Such close results could lead incumbents toward more acceptable voting patterns on business and fiscal issues. Furthermore, some of the challengers were newcomers and had done well enough to be encouraged to run again. Given the built-in advantage of incumbency, challengers had to run more than once to obtain the name recognition necessary for success. PAC I claimed some success in alerting contributors to the existence of other more complex measures of the worth of PAC giving.

2. PAC II is in the vanguard of those corporate PACs that have decided quite consciously to put the bulk of funds into support of challengers and open-seat contestants. It is not concentrating on winning access but seeks to help in campaigns where there is potential to contribute to philosophical change in the Congress. Naturally, in adopting such a strategy, one would have to be prepared for a high loss rate. PAC II does not shrink from giving statistics on win rates, but it places its stress elsewhere. PAC officers disseminate in their reports a voting record analysis, showing how PAC-supported winners and candidates whom the PAC unsuccessfully opposed have voted on a range of general business and industry-specific issues. There is clear-cut differentiation in relevant stands on the issues between the two kinds of candidates. The voting analysis underscores the point that PAC selections were good ones, motivated by a coherent philosophy, whether the candidates supported won or lost. It conveys to the PAC's constituency a clear message that the PAC can make good its claim to decide better on whom to support or oppose than individuals acting alone. Such presentations are also attractive adjuncts to PAC solicitation efforts.

Even in the absence of legal requirements, PACs wisely acknowledge their responsibility to report to their constituencies periodically on how they expend their funds. The quality of the reporting, however, differs widely. Much of it is narrowly focused on the data itself, without amplifying inter-

pretation and analysis. The prevalence of winners in the list of candidates is
the most widely cited index of PAC efficacy. A certain number of PACs,
however, provide examples of how reporting can be utilized as an opportunity to reinforce understanding of PAC purpose, demonstrate the consistency with which PAC guiding criteria have been applied in the actual
practice of giving, and even enlarge constituency understanding of some of
the realities of American politics.

Contributor Participation and Influence

The joining of the PAC by individual contributors represents, for most, an
extension of their participation in the body politic. To the act of voting they
now add a role in the financing of campaigns. But direct participation by individual contributors in the internal affairs of the PAC itself tends to be
limited. They are for the most part not active in the actual running of the
organization. They do not, for example, select the officers or the members
of the committees that administer the PAC, nor do they provide a heavy
flow of candidate recommendations to the selection committee.

Their participation in the PAC, if limited, is at the same time crucial.
Without their having made the choice in the first place to contribute funds,
there would be no PAC, and without sufficient and continuing response to
solicitations, there cannot be an effective PAC. Those who are active in the
running of PACs are well aware of this cardinal fact, and this means they
must constantly bear in mind possible reactions of contributors to decisions
(especially about candidate selection). The giving and possible withholding of
money by contributors confer influence and suggest that ignoring or disappointing expectations is always a serious matter for PAC decision makers.

The concentration of attention on the growth of corporate PACs, both
in numbers and funds, overlooks the fact that not all have been pursuing a
steady onward and upward course. Some, in their short organizational
lives, have already suffered sharp declines in numbers of contributors and
amounts raised. Some have lapsed into virtual inactivity or have raised in-
consequential amounts ("paltry PACs" by their own admission). Contributors can and do cease giving to the PAC. Much interview evidence from
PAC officers acknowledges that there is turnover of contributors. Fresh
solicitations may be required, because some contributors stop giving despite
payroll-deduction provisions. A number of PACs in the sample were
already planning to reorganize and revitalize their operations, because fund
raising had faltered or never really been started. The contributor constituency
shows signs that it is not captive, despite the conviction of some critics that
executives are dragooned into giving by the weight of social pressures they
are in no position to resist.

Executives may refrain from joining the PAC or drop out for a variety of reasons not related to disappointment with the way PAC money is being spent. But the possibility that they might do so has to be weighed by PAC officers and affects their decision making. In a variety of ways PAC officers, in their conduct of PAC affairs, reflect the influence that contributors exert through the ability to give or withhold funds. Almost universally, PAC officers choose to acknowledge their accountability to the contributors by reporting to them periodically, although the quality and depth of such reporting, as noted, vary widely. The reports of most PAC officers seek to establish the efficacy of the PAC by pointing to the high percentage of winning candidates that were selected. The point here is that officers concentrate on win rates out of a felt need to hold contributors and gain new ones. They are engaged in a constant selling and reselling of the PAC to their constituents, and the win rates seem the simplest and most direct way to establish that the money contributed has not been wasted. Reporting to constituents exposes the committee to possible complaints by contributors either about specific candidate selections or the whole trend and direction of PAC giving.

Although it is true that the flow of individual-contributor recommendations in most cases is hardly more than a trickle, it should not be assumed that committees have little knowledge of the political sentiments of their constituents. Communication between the committee and constituents takes place in a number of ways that are not dependent on formal procedure. Representatives of the contributors sit on the committees. Some committees have been composed specifically to give representation to a cross section of the executive population. PAC officers know many executives personally. They have a good deal of information about the politics of the contributors. In the interviews they repeatedly characterize the party affiliations and sympathies of the contributors. They may be well aware that the contributors are overwhelmingly Republican or include a mix of both parties. One PAC officer specifically acknowledged that his PAC was careful to make donations to candidates of both parties, because the political affiliations of the contributor group were mixed. PAC officers make it a point to know what the state of sentiment is among the contributors at the various plant locations of the corporation. They are in touch with plant managers or others who can brief them on how corporate executives regard the competing candidates in the races in their districts. Especially for hotly contested seats, where contributors may be expected to have strong feelings about the outcome, PAC officers take the trend of contributor sentiment into account in deciding whom to support. The study of split giving showed that a committee may engage in the practice on occasions when it disagrees with the trend of contributor sentiment in a given race or when it finds that the contributors are divided in their support of the candidates. In either case the committee's concern is to avoid the alienation of contributors.

No PAC that even remotely aims at effectiveness can afford to be widely out of touch with the donation preferences of its contributors. The most successful PACs are premised upon a strong rapport between committee and contributors and a shared commitment to PAC contribution criteria, even though the actual execution of the contribution strategy is left to PAC officers. The dependence of the PAC upon the support of contributors makes them a focal point of influence on PAC behavior, but this does not mean that committees automatically follow contributor preferences in candidate selection. Committees are usually disinclined to honor contributor recommendations that are considered grossly incompatible with the criteria set forth in the bylaws. More fundamentally, divergence between contributors and committees may arise because the latter do not think only of translating the ideological or partisan sentiments of contributors into candidate selections. Committees have to mediate between contributor preferences and PAC perception of corporate interests, and these do not always coincide. Auto-industry executives, for example, who are an important constituency of the Republican party in Michigan, may want to support only Republican candidates there, but those who run the auto PACs may feel obliged to give some support to incumbent liberal-labor Democrats who have rallied around the industry and have helped to fight its battles in Washington. Some officers of pragmatic PACs admit that they would attract more contributors and raise more money from executives if they were more ideologically oriented in their candidate selections. Nevertheless, they emphasize access to incumbents, because they believe that corporate interests are best served by following such a course. PACs are both constituency organizations and instruments of the corporations that sponsor them and defray their costs of operation. PAC officers have the complex task of thinking politically on behalf of the corporation while at the same time remaining responsively attuned to the contributor constituency whose funds they are spending.

Summary and Observations

The view that corporate PACs pursue an entirely independent existence, that their presence in the corporate environment is fortuitous, and that top management has little or no say in their affairs appears overstated. PACs are authorized by CEOs, because their activity is seen to be related to furthering corporate interests. The definition of PAC purpose and its implementation in a campaign-contribution strategy cannot be matters of indifference to corporate leadership. CEOs do not, in most cases, set the overall direction of PAC giving, but they will certainly have to acquiesce in the initiatives of those who do. Changes in solicitation policy require decisions that must ultimately be made by the CEO. Although the CEO in appointing PAC officers may frequently be ratifying the nominations of others, he will himself usually make the critical appointments of the one or two key officers to manage PAC affairs, and these key officers will serve as the CEO's communication link to the PAC.

If it goes too far to assert that corporations and their PACs are independent of each other, it would be a mistake as well to underestimate the elements of representativeness, voluntarism, and accountability that appear in the relations of the PAC to its constituency. The life blood of the PAC is the money raised from voluntary contributors, and significant constituency influence and opportunity for participation flow from this fact. It will not be easy to persuade those who argue that such contributions, by their nature, cannot be voluntary. But the evidence suggests that corporate PACs generally take pains to avoid tactics (even some that the law plainly permits) that could be perceived as coercive. The inconvenient fact for holders of the view that voluntarism is a myth and PAC giving is, in reality, indirect corporate giving is the large percentage of executives who decline to make any contributions or who drop out after having previously contributed. Corporate executives who are solicited do not seem to behave like organization men, and they show resistance to the pressures to give that some insist must be overwhelming.

The key group engaged most actively in the governance of the PAC in the case of major corporations tends to be public-affairs officers designated by the CEO. Their recommendations weigh heavily in campaign-contribution decisions. However, there is a significant number of PACs where nonspecialist amateurs chosen directly to represent the contributors play an active role in the making of campaign-contribution decisions and are not passive rubber stamps of the public-affairs officers who serve with them. In some instances, moreover, because both public-affairs officers and CEOs see the PAC as mainly about the political activation of executives, the public-affairs officers are careful to position themselves at a distance from the committees, and the key decisions are in the hands of nonspecialist representatives. Even when public-affairs officers designated by the CEOs play the leading part in PAC affairs, accountability to the contributors for what is done with their money is an obligation taken seriously, and real efforts to persuade the contributors that their money has been used effectively are made. Where preferences of contributors for particular candidates are expressed or known, they must be given careful attention.

The corporate PAC emerges from the examination of the evidence as a fairly complex, multidimensional organization. It is an amalgam in form, exhibiting strong elements of administration from above and connection with its parent corporation but at the same time manifesting some of the unmistakable features of a voluntary-constituency organization. The corporate PAC may not be a truly representative democracy, but neither is it entirely administered by corporate leadership or its agents under the cloak of a legitimizing myth of voluntarism.

5

PAC-Officer Perceptions and Attitudes

In this chapter an effort is made to extend the analysis one step further by examining the hypothesis that the variations in corporate PAC strategy previously discerned are in turn reflective of important differences in political attitude and outlook within the business community. It was possible in the seventy-one interviews to collect opinions for comparative purposes from PAC leaders in the following eight subject-matter areas: (1) intra-PAC criticisms of ideological and pragmatic strategies; (2) promotion of the free-enterprise system; (3) politicization of managerial employees; (4) parity with labor in the political arena; (5) public financing of congressional elections; (6) nonpartisanship; (7) PAC effectiveness; and (8) future PAC trends. The views expressed provide significant clues to the political thinking of those who lead corporate PACs.

Intra-PAC Criticisms of Ideological and Pragmatic Strategies

Eight pragmatic-PAC officers (32 percent) react adversely to what they perceive as efforts originating within the business community and from the Republican National Committee to influence corporate PACs to pursue a more unequivocally ideological trend in their campaign giving. They subscribe to the monthly information kit issued by the Business-Industry Political Action Committee (BIPAC) and take note without enthusiasm of its consistent policy of advocating support for Republican challengers. They received, as did officers of all corporate PACs, a letter from Justin Dart pressing them to cease support for antibusiness incumbents and to join in a drive to change the political balance in Congress.

Dart's approach to politics is generally unappealing to pragmatic-PAC officers. They assert that he wants to create a monolithic corporate-PAC movement that would seek to replace all liberal Democrats in the Congress with Republicans who share his political and economic views.

Pragmatic PACs are not about to commit their resources to further Dart's ideological positions or purposes. They resent his telling them that they are wrong in what they do, particularly so when he accuses them of undermining American business interests through support of antibusiness Democrats. Dart's PAC in their view is "an extension of himself," that is, it is his political mouthpiece, which he uses to advance his free-market philosophy. He and others like him ignore some very practical considerations about the real political world, when they urge others to follow their lead. They exhibit impatience with the pragmatic approach, because they do not look at the whole picture and thus miss the point that certain issues relating to a company take precedence when that company's interests are vitally impacted by the federal government. If companies that fall into this category were to make a long-term commitment to bring about a Republican Congress, they would face retribution from angry incumbents.

Pragmatic-PAC officers ask why PACs that are content with the present composition of Congress should trust ideological-PAC leaders who "are trying to run the show with someone else's dollars." In politics, extremists on the Left and Right are the most dangerous and do the most damage. This applies to overly zealous, partisan PACs that seek a new Congress. What these PACs really have in mind when they say that they want to change the composition of Congress is Republicans replacing Democrats. Those interviewed claim there is need for "new blood on both sides of the aisle—a lot of Republicans should go too." Ideological PACs in their opinion also overlook the fact that there are many incumbent Democrats who are reasonably probusiness. Should they continue on their present course, they are bound to offend both Democrats and the general public. The repercussions could trigger a far-reaching and adverse reaction against all corporate PACs.

Two of the pragmatic-PAC spokesmen (8 percent) agreed with Justin Dart's strictures on pragmatic-PAC strategy. They denounced their own PACs' support for liberal Democrats and vowed that this would not happen again. Significantly, their PACs switched to the ideological side in 1980.

Nine of the ideological-PAC officers (28 percent) are enthusiastic supporters of the Dart/BIPAC brand of politics. Two others (5 percent), though generally supportive, express reservations about Dart's highly partisan approach. For one thing, they say, there are many probusiness Democrats. For another, PAC contributors include Democrats and Independents; supporting only Republicans could destroy the PAC. Besides, there is a trend away from incumbents among business PACs. It is a natural, evolutionary development that grows as contributors gain understanding of the connection between business and politics. To impose an antiincumbent policy from the top could abort this development.

Four other ideological PACs (10 percent) deplored or were wary of what they consider zealots and activists of the Left and the Right, citing as examples Common Cause on the one hand and BIPAC on the other. (Two of them shifted to the pragmatic type in 1980.) Many companies, they elaborated, have to deal with Congress in a practical way. Such companies can be seriously hurt by taking controversial stands. Those who try to rally these companies to the ideological standard are not facing reality. This is not surprising, since CEOs like Justin Dart who set up and run PACs "tend to be politically naive and philosophical." PACs should strive for a balance between ideological goals and those that are attainable.

One of the four criticized BIPAC for having organized some of the more conservative PAC leaders into a group that meets and consults regularly. These officers, he claimed, are in touch with certain single-issue groups, such as the gun-control and right-to-life lobbies, and exchange suggestions about whom to support or oppose. This kind of right-wing-coalition politics is unfortunate. It goes beyond reasonable financing of conservative candidates, gives a poor image to business PACs, and could cause problems. The distribution of a list of particular politicians whom corporate PACs are urged not to support is not going to help either.

There is general agreement among ideological PACs that some of the criticisms lodged by Dart and BIPAC against the pragmatic approach are valid. They deplore PACs that care only about how incumbents treat their companies. A PAC should not contribute to a liberal Democrat solely because he is supportive of its company's interests. If there are employees and a company site in his district, his support is not a favor; it is an obligation. He should not be rewarded for this. Furthermore, why give an incumbent money because of one issue, if his record is otherwise totally antibusiness? What corporate PACs should be doing is not seeking favor in the Congress but looking for viable, probusiness candidates. Washington representatives who exercise too much influence in pragmatic-PAC contribution decisions also come in for a share of the criticism. One ideological-PAC interviewee, a Washington representative himself, lashed out at Washington representatives who boast about how much money they raise, the numbers of winners they pick, and their ability to influence incumbents.

Some of the criticisms aimed at those who follow the pragmatic path convey strong personal feelings. PACs engaged in split giving show, according to one respondent, "a complete lack of integrity." The same holds true for those who give indiscriminately to incumbents with antibusiness voting records. These PACs are "locked into a selfish pursuit of access," even though such a policy redounds to the detriment of the business community. "Access," observed one ideological critic, "can mean access to a turkey." PACs that underwrite liberal Democrats, warned another, "are feeding the alligators." A third used stronger language: "The bastards are contributing to the enemies of business."

Promoting the Free-Enterprise System

PAC officers, nourished on faith in business ideology, preach that their committees are working to help preserve the viability of the free-market economy. But, in the words of a PAC chairman, "criteria for contributions pit company interests against a probusiness philosophy, because the purpose of a PAC is to serve the interests of both the company and free enterprise." Under ordinary circumstances this dichotomy does not pose much of a problem for ideological PACs; their contributions are governed more by broad, philosophical considerations than by specific issues that bear upon the welfare of their companies. Ideological PACs, unlike those whose sole function is to advance the interests of their companies, bring to the world of politics a wider focus, one that encompasses their intent to change the tone and direction of government policy to one favorably oriented to business issues.

Ideological PAC officers tend to describe their work in behalf of free enterprise in apocalyptic terms. The problem, as they see it, is that too few members of Congress

> understand or are committed to the American business system. We prosper through our institutions of economic and political freedom. There's a need to get a greater number of congressmen to understand this. We're at a watershed. We have to take effective action to protect the business system, or it will be ruined by government interference.

The purer the ideology, the more likely the PAC to maintain a posture of supporting only candidates who favor the free-enterprise system. All PACs, in their opinion, should bend every effort to defeat those congressmen or those seeking congressional office who have antibusiness views. Those PACs that do not follow this line, that contribute instead to the enemies of free enterprise, said one such officer, "are prostituting themselves for selfish company interests."

Pragmatic PACS are just as eager to trumpet their commitment to the free-enterprise system. Their literature and cassettes abound with such statements as: "We need concerted action to elect men and women who believe in the market economy and who have the strength and will to stand firm against those who want increased government regulations and interference." Pragmatic-PAC officers also claim to weigh this consideration in their contribution decisions. Several maintain that their PACs would not contribute "to those who are philosophically opposed to us." However, many admit that free-enterprise considerations are secondary to the policy of promoting the interests of their company. Whether or not a candidate favors the free-market economy may be a criterion for contributions but guidelines on this point are not stringent. Efforts are made to screen out antibusiness candidates, although this is not a primary focus. Company interests are paramount, hence when business ideology contradicts those interests, the latter prevail. The spokesman for a railroad PAC explained why this is the case for his industry: "A railroad cannot feel fanatical about the free market. It is so heavily regulated and for so long. It wants a good business climate, and this means a favorable regulatory environment." Others say that their PACs support ideological liberals for what they do on behalf of the company, not for their public posture, or because there are so many of them.

Another interviewee went so far as to dismiss talk about free enterprise as irrelevant: "The company is committed to the preservation of the free enterprise system, whatever the hell that is, but money should go to the best politicians not just to ideologues who may give lip service to free enterprise."

Politicizing Managerial Employees

There is general agreement among those interviewed that a PAC provides a vehicle for participation in politics for management-level employees and that it contributes to their understanding of how politics works, heightens their concern with issues affecting their company or industry, and deepens their interest in politics. The PAC draws businessmen into the world of politics, many for the first time. In the past, management was not politically involved: "Their business was to run the business; politics was for the politicians." Now, thanks to PACs, they are learning that politics is too important to be left to the politicians. Therefore, more businessmen than ever before are politically active and contributing to campaigns.

The interviewees concur, too, that public-affairs programs designed to elevate the political awareness of business managers and to stimulate their participation in the political process are vital to the financial well being of most PACs, for they derive the bulk of their revenues from this constituency. PAC officers, in order to sell their program, must first address the task of political education, a task made especially formidable for those who run pragmatic PACs since they must convince employees that it is in their interests to support large numbers of prolabor, antibusiness Democratic incumbents. To this end, they emphasize that the PAC shares employee concerns for the free-enterprise system and that, since a corporation is, among other things, an aggregate of people with a large stake in the company the PAC represents "an investment on the part of the company in its managerial employees and vice versa." Government and politics are very much part of the business world and this fact profoundly affects employees, their companies, their careers, and their lives. Politically astute managers, that is, those who grasp the symbiotic nature of the company-employee relationship, readily make "the connection between their interests in the future of the company and what happens in the political arena." In short, a

PAC, by providing both company and employees with an effective political voice, serves the interests of each.

A number of those engaged in this educational campaign, credit their programs with having had a significant effect in raising the political consciousness of executives and with having imparted to PAC members a better understanding of how Congress works. Moreover, businessmen contributing money to their company's PAC take greater interest in politics.

Educational programs notwithstanding, pragmatic-PAC officers encounter widespread resistance to their solicitation campaigns from company managers, in particular those at middle or lower levels. In part they ascribe failure to elicit greater response from solicitees to Republican preferences of managers who reject the pragmatic considerations that go into decisions to contribute to liberal Democrats. The more partisan (that is, Republican) the solicitee, the more adamant his or her insistence that the PAC concentrate its funds on Republican candidates. Nine of the twenty-one pragmatic PACs soliciting below top management-level (43 percent) encountered this kind of resistance.

Ideological-PAC officers do not appear to share this problem. They cultivate a constituency group inherently receptive to the partisan thrust of their political commitments, and, for this reason, when they stress the voting records of incumbents, they anticipate that company employees will identify and work toward the defeat of those they oppose. Accordingly, efforts to politicize employees have brought an increase in Republican support with little if any grumbling about political philosophy. Managers of these PACs, to a much greater extent than those from the pragmatic group, speak glowingly of how employees, once connected with the PAC, become much more politically aware.

Employee political participation, to the pragmatic, means the contribution of money to the company PAC. For ideological PACs, too, "money comes when people finally decide to get interested in politics." But the ideological-PAC campaign to politicize managerial employees is linked to their efforts at altering the Congress. Thus while pragmatic-PAC officers, who are seeking access through contributions, equate donations with political participation, for representatives of 70 percent of the ideological PACs in the sample encouraging people to participate in politics relates to other political activities. A PAC, as they define it, is "a two-pronged vehicle—both equally important—to raise money and to involve our people in the political process." One interviewee whose company's credo says that employees should and must be involved in politics at all levels instructs solicitees, "if you're not going to get involved don't contribute." Another confided that his PAC was going to expand its solicitation universe from 364 to 10,000 "not to raise more money but to involve the maximum number of employees in the political process." Others make the same claim:

"We'd like to expand our PAC more in terms of manpower than money. We'd like to get more of our people involved in political campaigns."

For pragmatic officers, then, the PAC provides the means for the company to be heard; for ideological officers it affords business employees the same opportunity. It is "one of the most effective vehicles to generate individual participation in the political process to come along in a long time." Its primary emphasis, according to an ideological-PAC spokesman,

> is to stimulate interest in good government at every level. It's an on-going process of political education: monitoring the city council, meetings with politicians at brown bag luncheons. The effort at grass-roots involvement develops considerable interest in the government. It's an exciting thing and has excelled everyone's hopes.

Another interviewee developed the grass-roots theme more fully:

> Our first goal is to involve our people in the political process. Only about five percent of our time is devoted to fund raising and the distribution of funds; 95 percent is devoted to political education. Our philosophy is to encourage long-term understanding and continuing involvement in the political process.

Grass-roots participation takes the form of writing letters to candidates and incumbents, holding political-discussion meetings, inviting politicians to speak to employee groups, getting involved in campaigns. Business in the past was politically ineffective, because "for too long it left these matters to others." Now business is tapping the potential of employee involvement and the effects are already clear: Politically activated employees in plants throughout the country pressure and influence congressmen in their districts. Where once Common Cause and Congress Watch had the ear of Congress and it was difficult even to get a hearing, business, through its grass-roots effort, is reversing the situation.

Although both pragmatic and ideological PACs show commitment to politicizing managers, there is a significant difference. Pragmatic PACs concentrate on educating managers about the connection between the company's welfare and their own well being. These PACs must overcome, in the process, the Republican leanings of business managers. Ideological PACs, on the other hand, deal with a constituency inherently receptive to their partisan leanings. This enables them to seek not only donations, but also the active participation of constituents in congressional campaigns.

Corporate PACS as a Balance to Labor's Political Power

Corporate-PAC leaders on both sides of the ideological-pragmatic divide believe that organized labor until recently commanded majority votes in the

Congress for its programs because of its well organized support for pro-labor candidates. They perceive the growth of the corporate-PAC movement in recent years as having brought about "a salutary balance" to union political power. Formerly, when an imbalance existed between labor and business political contributions, congressmen were, in their view, unduly influenced by the unions. The prolabor majorities in both houses reflected, in part, an awareness by congressmen that funds would be denied if they voted contrary to the union point of view. This is no longer the case because the emergence of corporate PACs provides congressional candidates with an alternative to labor money. This, in turn, has helped to create a political environment in which congressmen possess greater latitude to exercise their own judgments.

Representatives of only seven of the pragmatic PACs in the sample (28 percent) mentioned the subject of labor politics, and only three of them expressed apprehension about labor's political influence, evidence that, among this group of PAC leaders, political competition with labor does not have high priority. Moreover, those who did voice concern focused on the earlier state of affairs, when substantially more money was collected from unions than was contributed by individual businessmen. They are satisfied that Congress, when it removed the barriers to the formation of corporate PACs, provided the means to correct the imbalance.

Some of those who did not speak out on the issue represent firms that are not objects of serious organizing efforts by unions, and this may account for their silence. But there are others from companies that employ scores of thousands of union workers who also do not overly emphasize the union theme or that see labor not as a political opponent but as an ally. Such is the case for this railroad-PAC manager:

> Our company is very highly unionized. Inflammatory rhetoric about unions is absent. Unions in the railroad industry are very supportive. The welfare of the industry is a shared concern. We might support some of the same candidates that rail unions support.

There are business leaders, he continued, who want corporate PACs to attack unions or who would like to see them assume the ideological commitment of union PACs. This does not make sense when union and company interests do not conflict. It is to the mutual advantage of labor and management to coalesce in the face of a common threat. They should heed the example of the railroad union which, in a declining industry, allies itself with management "in trying to preserve and extend utilization of the rails."

Fear of retrenchment or company failure is not the only thing that drives labor and management together. A pragmatic-PAC chairman, discussing his experiences in labor-management relations, observed that unions, like corporations, exist in a pluralistic world. He cited his company (a large, prospering manufacturing firm) as an example of how unions and management collaborate on issues that impinge on the welfare of both. Relations between union and company are harmonious because "we find ways to share in one another's power through coalition." The company and its union presented a joint petition to Congress calling for import quotas, a proposal that other companies and unions vehemently oppose.

Sixteen ideological-PAC officers (40 percent) talked about labor politics; thirteen cast labor in the role of adversary. (The three who did not echoed the opinion of some pragmatic officers that company unions "are shoulder to shoulder with us" on industry-related issues.) The great majority, however, see no reason for a truce with organized labor. Labor showed no interest in parity when it enjoyed the political advantage. Now that Congress has given members of the corporate community a role in the electoral system, this right should be fully exploited to expand the political influence of business.

Corporate PACs by closing the gap between themselves and labor PACs have sparked what one respondent calls "hysterical opposition" on the part of organized labor and other antibusiness groups like Congress Watch and Common Cause, which cry for the revision of the campaign finance law solely to slow the progress of business PACs. There was no criticism by the media, academia, or the liberal spectrum of the body politic when labor monopolized the process. Now that corporate PACs have become competitive, critics tag them special-interest groups. They decry the sums of money that business raises while overlooking the amounts that union PACs collect. They fail also to remark on the fact that union-PAC spending favors Democrats ten-to-one as compared to the two-to-one margin that corporate PACs accord Republican candidates. The media, in particular, pursue what was termed a double-standard approach to the issue of campaign donations:

> The media have developed a conspiratorial theory with regard to corporate PACs. They see nothing wrong with labor or environmentalists' involvement in politics. We don't criticize labor unions and their money. They ought to do it. That's what representative democracy is all about.

Another ideological-PAC officer maintained that corporate-PAC giving is a "highly defensive" response to union giving and predicted that if unions would end their political activities "we would quit also." (Ironically, unions, alarmed by the rising flow of corporate-PAC dollars into congressional races, say the same thing.) Ideological-PAC managers, regardless of whether or not they believe that unions have too much power, see much in the record of labor politics that is worthy of emulation. Unions, for example, have evolved a system of candidate development; that is, they dispense seed money to promising individuals so that they may run for office. Even if the newcomer loses the first time, he gains experience and creates a public image that will enhance his chance for victory the next time. Those corporate-PAC managers who want new faces in Congress will do well to adopt this technique. And just as unions spend money on the political education of workers, "We, too, need to do more than just get our people to give money." One way would be for business PACs to adopt the union practice of enlisting volunteers to serve in political campaigns. By one estimate the average full-time campaign worker's worth is around $10,000 or twice the amount that the law permits a PAC to contribute to a candidate's campaign.

There are those operating ideological PACs who see in the declining political power of labor and the Democratic party an opportunity to increase business influence in Congress. Corporate PACs, according to one, are not to blame for the decline; labor and the Democratic party have only themselves to blame. They are out of step with rank-and-file workers who no longer believe in big government and who are growing more conservative. It behooves corporate PACs to take advantage of the situation and to move into the political vacuum left by the waning powers of labor and the Democratic party in order to expand their influence.

A number of pragmatic-PAC managers deem such a policy either unwise or likely to prove self-defeating. Corporations resorted to the PAC device primarily to compete with labor on equal terms, a goal that they have already reached. Labor, in spite of its vigorous and long-standing use of the PAC device, is losing its power in Congress, a demonstration that political funding has its limitations. Because of rapid growth in numbers and wealth, the resources of corporate PACs may soon so far exceed those of labor's PACs that it could frighten the public and produce countermeasures.

Public Financing of Congressional Campaigns

The defeat in committee in 1979 of H.R.1, a proposal for public financing of congressional campaigns, did not lay that issue to rest. Opponents of corporate PACs like Common Cause and COPE continue to push it as a desirable alternative to funding by special-interest groups. Even within the confines of corporate PACs themselves, there are those who favor public funding. However, twenty-two of the twenty-five interviewees who discussed the subject were opposed, some adamantly, others less so. Some opponents believe such a law will significantly diminish the ability of PACs to provide financial support for political candidates. One officer went so far as to assert that federal financing "could have meant the demise of PACs, which was the intent of the bill's proponents." Others, somewhat less pessimistic, see PACs continuing to operate within a public-funding system, albeit with their effectiveness reduced. A pragmatic-PAC officer expected that, in the event such legislation passes, corporate PACs will be forced to funnel their money into primary races, a potential development that he viewed with alarm, since PACs "cannot make proper judgments on primary candidates." On the other hand, an ideological-PAC officer found the prospect of PACs having to concentrate their spending in primaries less than frightening. In his opinion, corporate PACs, simply by shifting the balance of their funds to "targets of opportunity" in primary campaigns, will remain as influential as ever. Another possibility, he foresaw, is that they might seriously consider making independent expenditures.

Another reason for opposition to H.R.1 was that the bill gave incumbents a head start in their bid for reelection instead of taking steps to neutralize advantages incumbents enjoy. One of these advantages is that incumbents can raise money more easily than can their opponents, and thus they will more easily qualify for matching funds.

Two respondents challenged this idea contending that the answer to the question of whether government funds benefit incumbents depends on the circumstances that prevail in a particular district. The safer the district, the less likely a serious challenge, but in districts where the incumbent belongs to one party and a majority of his constituents to another, public funding will encourage challenges. Rank-and-file Democrats in the House as well as Republicans were aware of the snares contained within the proposal, as evidenced by the broad spectrum of Democrats and Republicans who, for different reasons, joined in committee to defeat it: the Democrats because they feared availability of taxpayer money might initiate challenges; the Republicans because they perceived H.R.1 as an incumbent-protection bill.

Some respondents opposed federally financed elections on philosophical grounds. "It's a bad idea," said one, "to use taxpayers' money to help get people elected who as a citizen you may not wish to support." "We need people involvement," said another, not a system that would allow "an idiot to get his hands on tax money." As private money goes out popular input into the political process soon follows. Witness what happened when public funding was introduced into presidential campaigns. The spirit of voluntarism, so pronounced in the 1952 campaign, disappeared by 1976 to be replaced by professional campaign organizations. One ideological-PAC officer labelled the campaign for a public-funding law "a conspiracy against good government and democratic voluntary participation." The right to contribute money to candidates of one's own choice "ranks equally with the right to vote." To deprive citizens of that right would constitute "an atrocious violation" of freedom of choice.

Two of the pragmatic-PAC respondents warned that PACs that become overly militant in their party-ideological stance "play into the hands of federal-funding advocates." No ideological PAC officer voiced similar misgivings. Nor did any ideological-PAC officer support the concept of publicly funded campaigns. By contrast, three pragmatic-PAC interviewees either favored the adoption of a public-funding law or were not opposed to it. One advocated public funding because "the strain of collecting and controlling PAC money is a pain in the neck." Furthermore, PAC financing of candidates is self-defeating, not because it threatens to pollute the political arena with easily available money as its more hostile critics charge, but because "it's a game in which the ante goes up all the time." Congressmen, this respondent believes, "think there's no end to the money, and their importuning will continue to expand." Those PACs that do not give or give less will find doors starting to close.

Nonpartisanship

PAC officers without exception describe their organizations as nonpartisan, by which they mean that a candidate's party affiliation does not automatically determine the decision whether or not to contribute to his campaign. Nevertheless, differing concepts of what constitutes nonpartisan behavior conform to PAC grouping along the ideological-pragmatic divide.

When asked, representatives of ideological PACs defend their one-sided support for Republican candidates on the grounds that, outside of the South, probusiness Democrats are an endangered species. They prefer that their PACs not be labelled Republican, but there are few sympathetic Democrats outside the South. One interviewee acknowledged that

> our support for so many Republicans might make it seem that big business and Republicans are allies. But we are not a party PAC; we're an issues PAC. It's true our PAC gave to a preponderance of Republicans. We looked for suitable Democrats but couldn't find them.

A candidate's political philosophy, not his party label, guides ideological-PAC contribution decisions, but the fact that more Republicans than Democrats are for free enterprise accounts for the disparity, in party terms, of their overall contribution record. In the ideological scheme of things, the acceptable Democrat must carry the credentials of an unequivocally conservative, probusiness advocate, a demand that eliminates all but a handful of non-Southern Democratic incumbents.

A PAC, as some of the ideological purists interpret it, has "a moral contract" with its contributors: "It stands for something; it would violate that moral contract, if it were to give money to liberals." PACs should not function as "lobbying devices." Ultimately, what ideological PACs want is a better Congress, an aim that goes to the heart of the matter of nonpartisanship, for what they mean by better, even though few mention it, is a Congress controlled by Republican majorities.

Pragmatic PAC officers attribute their willingness to support disproportionate numbers of incumbent Democrats to their influential positions in Congress. For the typical pragmatic PAC, party affiliation is irrelevant. What is relevant is "the committees that members sit on." Pragmatic PACs intend to continue to support incumbents who, though "not sound on many issues, vote right in committees on issues of salient importance to the company." A few confess to a certain amount of embarrassment caused by those instances when their PACs gave money to congressmen with otherwise unfavorable voting records, and others profess an affinity for viable Republicans and conservative Democrats. Most, however, are not promoting any philosophy, and most also sublimate whatever political preferences they personally entertain with acceptance of a contribution policy that assigns top priority to candidates who sympathize with the interests of their companies and are in a position to aid those interests. The few who insist that they share with the ideologicals the desire to aid Republican candidates admit that this is not a primary concern when their PACs make their contribution decisions. It is access to Congress that draws pragmatic-PAC support, and if those who are willing to listen to company representatives happen to be liberal Democrats, so be it. As for nonviable Republicans, they need not apply for PAC funds.

From the pragmatic standpoint, PACs that get too involved in partisan politics risk countermeasures. Besides, since companies must deal with political leaders on both sides of the aisle, a policy of supporting all Republicans is self-defeating, especially so for companies that operate in areas where Democrats control the political system. Furthermore, according to a pragmatic-PAC spokesman, it is not clear that business does better under Republicans. In fact, there are businesses that "have done very well under Democratic regimes in spite of all the rhetoric."

In sum, the more ideological a PAC, the deeper its commitment to a Republican takeover of the Congress, and this dictates a partisan contribution-policy. On the other side, the more pragmatic a PAC, the higher the proportion of its contributions going to Democrats. The direction of the flow, however, is governed not by party preference but by the presence in large numbers of Democrats in key posts within the Congress. If Republicans were to occupy these positions, they would receive the same support. They are nonpartisan because, in reality, they are apolitical.

PAC Effectiveness

Over 90 percent of the interviewees regard their own PACs or PACs in general as effective, and they offered a number of reasons why they believe this to be the case. As might be expected, 72 percent of the pragmatic PACs pointed to the establishment of good relations in Congress as the prime test of effectiveness. Half that number (36 percent) opined that their PACs have helped to politicize company employees (the second most frequently cited indicator).

Comparable figures for ideological PAC officers—33 percent and 45 percent respectively—underscore the different outlooks and emphases that prevail among PAC leaders as to what constitutes an effective PAC. For pragmatics, opening doors in Congress—the *sine qua non* for their committees—overshadows all other considerations, a fact that accounts for why so many of them equate access with accomplishment; but for ideological-PAC staff, activating managerial employees ties in with their efforts to establish a business-oriented Congress, and this outweighs access in their assessment of PAC effectiveness. Another indicator: 20 percent of the ideological PAC officers opposed on philosophical grounds the policy of contributing money in order to be heard in Congress. Not surprisingly, 70 percent of the ideologicals specified that corporate PACs are influencing legislative and election results and, therefore, are making headway toward their primary goal, a Congress reconstituted along philosophically compatible lines.

No pragmatic-PAC officer expressed any doubts about contributing just to be heard, nor did any of them mention change in the composition of Congress among their accomplishments. Twenty-four percent did remark that corporate PACs in the aggregate have contributed to a shift in attitude in Congress towards a more probusiness stance, but an equal number scoffed at the idea that PACs can act in concert, given the "collision of varying business interests." They were equally dubious that PAC money can determine the way congressmen vote or that PAC spending, even in the aggregate, is significant when framed in the perspective of the amounts pouring into congressional campaigns from other sources.

Pragmatic-PAC officers appear more sensitive to the relationship between the size of a PAC and its relative effectiveness. Proportionately, five times as many pragmatic as ideological PACs (40 percent to 8 percent) felt that contributions to candidates are too small to influence legislative or election results. "It's difficult to gauge the overall impact of PACs on Congress," observed one, "since the amounts are still small potatoes." Another 28 percent were struck by the irony of their committee's relative penury as compared to the enormous assets of their companies. According to them limited resources narrow their contribution targets; increased revenues would enable them to implement a more fully developed and coherent contribution strategy. On the question of just what that strategy would be if sufficient funds were available, most say they would channel more money into the campaigns of congressmen who seem potentially helpful to their companies. A couple of them, however, asserted that they want to raise more money so they can support more nonincumbents and defeat particular incumbents. No ideological-PAC spokesman said that financial considerations affected the direction of giving.

Future Trends

Spokesmen for fifty-four corporate PACs in the sample commented on plans and anticipated trends for their committees or for corporate PACs in general. Their remarks were directed mainly to expectations concerning internal and external growth and to the potential impact that PACs might have on the political process.

On the subject of PAC growth, of the thirty-three ideological-PAC administrators who discussed future trends, twenty-six (79 percent) expected continuing growth. Most of them planned to raise more money and increase the number of participants by refining or invigorating solicitation methods, by nurturing, through political-education programs, grass-roots organizations composed of managerial volunteers, and by expanding their solicitation universes. Several thought that solicitation should be treated as a marketing venture, one in which "we are going to have to sell the whole notion of the political process to our employees the way we sell our products." According to another ideological-PAC officer, the potential for growth in numbers is virtually unlimited, since the vast majority of the nation's corporations have not as yet formed PACs. Moreover, once a PAC "establishes a culture" that enables managerial employees to grasp the significance of the relationship between business, government, and politics, participation and revenue levels will rise. "What we're trying to do," explained an interviewee, "is gauged to the long term—the success of our PAC will come from heightening and sustaining the political awareness of our people."

Four ideological PACs proposed extending solicitation to a lower level of managerial employees, two from top management to all levels (from Category A to Category C), one from top to middle (from Category A to Category B), and one from middle to lower (from Category B to Category C). (By comparison, no pragmatic PAC intended to solicit at a lower level.)

Not all ideological-PAC interviewees who agreed on growth prospects unreservedly welcomed the trend. Some worried that too many PACs might start raising too much money. "There is an unfortunate mentality at work," observed one, "that if raising $50,000 is good, raising $100,000 is better." If PACs are too successful, public relations would be damaged. People would grow increasingly alarmed and pressure would mount to curb or abolish PACs.

Others, however, denounced as "populist demagogy" the idea that corporate PACs laden with money will overwhelm the political process. Since

campaigns are costly, candidates must seek funds from a broad base of contributors, not from a single source such as corporate PACs which, in any
case, lack the resources to meet the overall costs of campaigns. Corporate
PACs were responsible for only 4 percent of all contributions to congressional candidates in 1978. They could easily double their portion of total
contributions without cause for alarm. Finally, since the law prohibits coercion and places limits on giving, they predict that corporate PAC expenditures will remain relatively modest.

Five of the thirty-three ideological respondents (15 percent) either
planned no change in solicitation procedures or perceived serious limits to
future growth. (Two others did not mention growth.) Those doubtful of
future growth reasoned that companies that have already rejected the idea
of a PAC will not change their stand. Also, PACs, having achieved a
balance with labor, are not likely to go to an opposite extreme by seeking to
bring about imbalance in their own favor. Even if they were so inclined, it
should be remembered that contributions are voluntary; thus PACs must
depend upon the good will of employee contributors whom they cannot afford to offend with excesses, either in the solicitation or contribution areas.
Finally, there is no guarantee that PACs will be around forever. They exist
at the sufferance of Congress, a condition that stems from the fact that incumbents feel they are getting support from them. To undermine that conviction is to court disaster.

Twelve of the twenty-one pragmatic-PAC respondents (57 percent) expected their PACs to raise more money. "Our PAC is scrawny," said one,
"because our solicitation methods are antiseptic." He, like the others,
planned to improve solicitation techniques in order to bring in more money.
Only two of the group predicted an upward trend for the corporate-PAC
movement as a whole.

Six from the pragmatic group (29 percent) envisioned little prospect for
growth within their own PACs. Two (both Category A PACs) professed
themselves satisfied that their committees could accomplish their ends without further expansion. Another two saw little opportunity for growth,
because the amount of company money available for administering the
PAC was insufficient to provide the staffing essential for effective solicitation campaigns. A fifth did not anticipate significant changes, since his
PAC's solicitation policy is well-established; and the sixth asserted that his
PAC, in response to negative criticism from solicitees, would keep the numbers solicited quite restricted.

Three other pragmatic-PAC respondents (14 percent), although cheer-
ful about prospects for their own committees, predicted that corporate-
PAC growth, both in numbers and revenues, would taper off, just as labor
PACs did. They saw no danger of corporate PACs taking over the political
system. Those who believe otherwise fail to consider how many employees

are solicited and how many do not give. Moreover, the law limits a PAC to a maximum contribution of $5,000 to a candidate's campaign; and the public-disclosure provision of the law inhibits the amounts that individuals are willing to give. If PACs "stay in their place," stated one respondent, they will do well, but if they become too partisan and aggressive or if they try to pressure people into giving, "they'll lose out in the long run."

Concerning political impact, the significance of PAC growth, according to PAC boosters, is that, with increased numbers and revenues, PAC influence will spread. No longer will they have to concentrate on just a few candidates for want of money; from surplus funds will come the means to widen the focus of giving.

Twenty-five of the ideological-PAC respondents (76 percent) envisaged PACs performing an increasingly important political role. Eleven of this group expect that growing numbers of PACs will close ranks behind the drive to attain a probusiness Congress. Prior to 1980, when PACs were at the infancy stage, many contributed to Democratic incumbents. But as PACs mature, they will shift heavily toward Republicans and nonincumbents. PACs are the wave of the future, and in the future there will be greater unity among them. The break down of the Democratic party presents a splendid opportunity that PACs can exploit and thus turn the political direction of the country around. They are, it is believed, "the instrument for change that must take place over the next few years." Accordingly, each election will see more venturesome expenditures of corporate PAC funds.

Some ideological-PAC officers asserted that politically educating and activating company managers takes precedence over raising more money because of the political influence that large numbers of committed business personnel will exercise. No pragmatic-PAC officer made this claim. On the other hand, other ideological officers warn that PAC potential is too large and that they should avoid becoming disproportionate. Unless they exercise self-discipline, they will provoke retaliation such as a public-funding law. Others took an opposite stand, pointing to inherent limitations on their power. The need to siphon PAC money into state legislative campaigns will absorb expanding PAC resources. Contributions by different PACs to incumbent Democrats and their Republican challengers cancel each other out. PACs are not monolithic in perceptions and attitudes and can have a healthy, pluralizing effect. PACs are dependent upon their base of voluntary support, and the PAC movement must avoid actions that could turn contributors against it.

Twelve pragmatic PAC respondents (57 percent) presumed that PACs will have an increasing political impact. In the opinion of one, "the corporate PAC device is slowing government regulation down, and this will improve the economy through greater efficiency and lower prices. The American consumer will benefit." Another cited the support of liberal

Democrats for public funding as evidence that PACs are gaining momentum. This officer forecast the emergence of the "boll weevil" Democrat-Republican coalition in Congress, basing his prediction on the supposition that the dramatic rise in available corporate-PAC funds will render Democratic congressmen far less responsive to their leadership. Another pragmatic officer voiced concern that there might be such a thing as too much success. She feared that PACs that are "too slick and high pressured" might eventually dominate the PAC movement. There are others who run PACs, she added, who share her concern.

Three pragmatic-PAC officers (14 percent) rejected the idea that PACs are going to have an increasingly important effect on the political system. One of them, who predicted the shift to Republicans in 1980, said that the mood of the nation, not PACs, is moving voters toward the Republican party. PACs cannot transform the American political process: "We ride a log down the stream, but we can't control the stream." Those who think otherwise are deluded. A more likely development is that the demands of candidates will become inordinate. Already congressmen are importuning for money in off-years either for their next campaign or to pay off debts on their last election. They believe there is no end to corporate PAC money. This will result in a counterproductive exercise in that not giving or giving less will diminish access.

The interview data illustrate that buoyancy about growth prospects and the vision of an increasingly important political role for corporate PACs are much more pronounced among ideological-PAC officers than among the others. Eleven out of the thirty-three ideological-PAC respondents foresee wayward pragmatic PACs joining the movement to elect a probusiness Congress. At the same time, there is prevalent disbelief that PACs will continue to multiply indefinitely in numbers and revenues or that they will dominate the political system.

Conclusion

The interview data make clear that not all pragmatic-PAC leaders share the same perceptions and attitudes about PAC matters; they show also that ideological officers are not all partisan ideologues, nor are all pragmatic officers unconcerned about Democratic influence in the Congress. On the contrary, one finds in the data considerable overlapping in outlook among officers on both sides of the ideological-pragmatic divide. For example, lukewarm pragmatics apologize for their committee's support for large numbers of Democrats; and moderate ideologicals frown on their more intensely committed peers and, like pragmatics, warn against the dangers inherent in zealous partisanship.

At the same time, however, the interviewees exhibited in their conversations important differences in perceptions and attitudes in the eight areas examined. As might be expected, those who lead pragmatic PACs for the most part are comfortable working with the established political balance and demonstrate little interest in tinkering with the status quo in Congress. A PAC, in their opinion, is effective primarily because it establishes contacts in the Congress. Accordingly, most (but not all) oppose public funding of campaigns that would inhibit this advantage. Neither organized labor nor the Democratic party are considered particularly threatening; in fact, moderate Democrats are to be preferred to Republicans who are "to the right of Franco." They are satisfied that labor no longer holds the upper hand in the political arena and see no need to upset the balance of power that currently exists between labor and business PACs. Their idea of a politically active managerial employee is one who contributes to the PAC, not someone enrolled in the ranks of Republican activists. Since it costs far less to establish and maintain access than to replace incumbents with newcomers, pragmatic PACs, though not averse to increased revenues, display little interest in implementing policies that would guarantee high financial growth in the future.

Pragmatics see a pluralistic political world where cooperation and compromise get better results than challenge and conflict. Not for them New Deal-style political wars, pitting government, labor, and the Democrats against business and the Republican party. Indeed, some pragmatics hold that all would benefit if business, labor, and government were to harness themselves to a joint endeavor to promote prosperity, a vision that is impossible to reconcile to the free-enterprise ideal. But pragmatics are less interested in philosophical consistency than they are in political effectiveness as they measure it.

They decry business leaders like Justin Dart and organizations like BIPAC for their "hit list" approach to politics, considering them intemperate and single-minded partisans whose excesses could bring public and congressional outrage down on all their heads. Topping the pragmatic list of perceived ideological sins is the all-out offensive to change the composition of Congress. Why, pragmatics ask, mix partisan politics with business, when it is bound to stir potentially harmful reactions?

On the ideological side, access to congressmen is a secondary consideration. Most pursue it, but only to a limited extent. As is the case with the pragmatics, most ideologicals equate PAC effectiveness with their primary goal. What they are seeking is a probusiness Congress; hence they are not interested in striking a balance with labor in the political arena. They want victory over labor, the ultraliberals who want to snuff out the growing power of corporate PACs by extending public funding to congressional elections, and congressmen who consistently vote against the interests of business.

Claims of nonpartisanship notwithstanding, the ideologicals want to replace these Democrats with profree-enterprise newcomers who, they readily admit, would mostly be Republicans. Business managers will play an important part in the effort to achieve this victory, once they are politically activated. All this will take time and more resources than are now available, which is why ideological PACs are more future- and growth-oriented than the others.

Ideologicals tend to view the political world in Manichaean terms. It is a world in which the American business system is locked in a long-term struggle with enemies such as the media, academia, Common Cause, Congress Watch, organized labor, and the liberal wing of the Democratic party. And where pragmatics castigate them for endangering the whole PAC system with their single-minded pursuit of a Republican Congress, they reciprocate by accusing the pragmatics of undermining the cause of business with their indiscriminate support of liberal enemies.

The interview data suggest that the two broad and divergent streams of corporate-PAC giving reflect significant differences in perceptions and attitudes and, ultimately, in political standpoints and outlooks within that sector of the business community commonly referred to as Big Business. Both outlooks flow from a conservative source, but they represent two distinctly different kinds of conservatism: the moderate, centrist, and accommodationist approach of the pragmatics; and the more militant, rigid, principle-directed brand of New Right politics of the ideologicals.

Notes

Chapter 1

1. Federal Election Commission, Press Release, January 17, 1982.

2. United States Code 431-455 (1976 and supplement III, 1979).

3. Herbert E. Alexander, "The Obey-Railsback Bill: Its Genesis and Early History," in *Symposium: Political Action Committees and Campaign Finance,* Tom Scribner, ed., *Arizona Law Review* 22 (1980): 653-665; U.S. Congress, House, Committee on House Administration, *Public Financing of Congressional Elections: Hearings on H.R. 1,* 96th Cong., 1st sess., March 15-27, 1979, pp. 2-122.

4. "Directory of the 500 Largest U.S. Industry Corporations," *Fortune* (May 19, 1979), pp. 268-295; "Directory of the Second 500 Largest U.S. Industrial Corporations, *Fortune* (June 18, 1979), pp. 156-184; "Directory of the Largest U.S. Nonindustrial Companies," *Fortune* (July 16, 1979), pp. 156-170; Edwin M. Epstein, "Business and Labor under the Federal Election Campaign Act of 1971," in *Parties, Interest Groups, and Campaign Finance Laws,* Michael J. Malbin, ed., (Washington, D.C.: American Enterprise Institute for Policy Research, 1980), p. 128.

5. *Politikit* (Washington, D.C.: Business-Industry Political Action Committee, May 1979), pp. 36-37.

Chapter 2

1. Maxwell Glen, "At the Wire, Corporate PACs Come Through for the GOP," *National Journal* 11 (1979):174-177; Federal Election Commission, Press Release, May 10, 1979.

2. Phyllis S. McGrath, *Redefining Corporate-Federal Relations* (New York: Conference Board, 1977), p. 54.

3. *Wall Street Journal,* October 26, 1978, p. 26.

4. *New York Times,* August 19, 1979; IV, 5.

5. McGrath, *Corporate-Federal Relations,* p. 55; Dart letter summarized by PAC officers in interviews with authors.

6. Interview with Stevenson Walker, Public Affairs Council, January 12, 1979.

7. David Cohen, "The Special Interest Money Flood," *Citizen Participation* 1 (1979):1-12; Representative John Anderson, *Hearings on H.R. 1,* p. 217; and Interview with Victor Kamber, AFL-CIO, January 14, 1979.

8. Paul Weyrich, Committee for the Survival of a Free Congress, January 11, 1979; McGrath, *Corporate-Federal Relations,* p. 55.

9. Xandra Kayden, "The Impact of the Federal Election Campaign Act upon Political Action Committees," in *An Analysis of the Impact of the Federal Election Campaign Act, 1972-78,* a Report by the Campaign Finance Study Group to the Committee on House Administration (Cambridge, Mass.: Institute of Politics, John F. Kennedy School of Government, Harvard University, 1979), pp. 8-9.

10. U.S. Congress, House, *Congressional Record,* 96th Cong., 1st sess., 1979, 125: 9261-9305.

11. Kayden, *An Analysis of the Impact of the Federal Election Campaign Act, 1972-78,* pp. 2-3.

12. Michael J. Malbin, "Campaign Financing and 'Special Interests'," *Public Interest* 56 (Summer 1979), p. 34.

13. "How Special-Interest Groups Rate Representatives," *Congressional Quarterly Weekly,* June 2, 1979, pp. 1068-69.

14. Maxwell Glen, "The PACs are Back, Richer and Wiser, to Finance the 1980 Elections," *National Journal* 11 (1979): 1982-84.

15. McGrath, *Corporate-Federal Relations,* p. 55.

16. Interview with Stevenson Walker, January 12, 1979.

17. Malbin, "Campaign Financing," p. 35.

18. Michael J. Malbin, "Labor, Business, and Money-A Post Election Analysis," *National Journal* 9 (1977):412-417; Charles E. Lindblom, *Politics and Markets* (New York: Basic Books, 1977), pp. 170-200.

19. Edwin M. Epstein, "Dimensions of Corporate Power," in *Selected Major Issues in Business' Role in Modern Society* (Los Angeles, Calif.: Graduate School of Management, U.C.L.A., 1973), pp. 269-357; Lindblom, *Politics and Markets,* p. 170.

Chapter 3

1. Edwin M. Epstein, "The Business PAC Phenomenon: An Irony of Electoral Reform," *Regulation* (May-June 1979), p. 39; Bernadette A. Budde, "Business Political Action Committees," in Malbin, ed., *Parties, Interest Groups, and Campaign Finance Laws,* pp. 9-10.

2. Epstein, "Business and Labor," in Malbin, ed., *Parties, Interest Groups, and Campaign Finance Laws,* pp. 117, 143-146.

3. Clark MacGregor, "Commentaries," pp. 207-208; and Epstein, "Business and Labor;" p. 144 in Malbin, ed., *Parties, Interest Groups, and Campaign Finance Laws.*

4. Irving Kristol, *Two Cheers for Capitalism* (New York: Basic Books, 1978), pp. 146-150.

5. "Summary Report of the 1976 Political Action Committee Survey," in *Guidelines for Corporate Political Action Committees*

(Washington, D.C.: Chamber of Commerce of the United States, 1977); Public Affairs Council's 1978 Political Action Committee Survey, June 29, 1978; and McGrath, *Corporate-Federal Relations*, p. 50.

6. *Dollar Politics*, 3rd ed. (Washington, D.C.: Congressional Quarterly Inc., 1982), p. 42.

7. Curtis C. Sproul, "Corporations and Unions in Federal Politics: A Practical Approach to Federal Election Law Compliance," in Scribner, ed., *Symposium: Political Action Committees and Campaign Finance*, pp. 481-482; Federal Election Commission Regulations, April 1977, pp. 76-78.

8. *Federal Election Commission Regulations*, April 1977, p. 74.

9. *Federal Election Commission Determination and First General Counsel's Report to the Federal Election Commission on the Complaint of the International Association of Machinists, et. al.*, December 13, 1979, pp. 4-11.

10. *Hearings on H.R. 1*, p. 219.

11. *Wall Street Journal*, August 15, 1978, p. 1.

12. William H. Whyte, *The Organization Man* (New York: Simon and Shuster, 1956).

Chapter 4

1. John C. Perham, "The New Zest of the Corporate PACs," *Dun's Review*, February 1980, pp. 50-52.

2. Philip Crane, "The Constituency of PACs," *Business and Society Review*, Summer 1980, p. 6.

3. Donald M. Kendall, Commencement Address, Babson College *Alumni Bulletin*, Summer 1980, p. 5.

4. *Plaintiff's Motion for Summary Judgment, International Association of Machinists and Aerospace Workers* v. *Federal Election Commission*, U.S. District Court for the District of Columbia, pp. 6-9.

5. Sproul, "Corporations and Unions in Federal Politics" in Scribner, ed., *Symposium: Political Action Committees and Campaign Finance*, pp. 492-93.

6. Interview with Stevenson Walker, January 12, 1979.

7. Bernadette A. Budde, "Business Political Action Committees," pp. 11-12; and Edwin M. Epstein, "Business and Labor," p. 133, in Malbin, ed., *Parties, Interest Groups, and Campaign Finance Laws*.

8. Epstein, "Business and Labor," p. 127.

9. Federal Election Commission, Press Release, January 17, 1982.

10. Herbert E. Alexander, *Money in Politics* (Washington, D.C.: Public Affairs Press, 1972), p. 181.

11. Alan Berlow and Laura B. Weiss, "Energy PACs: Potential Power

in Elections," *Congressional Quarterly Weekly*, November 3, 1979, p. 2458.

12. Irving S. Shapiro, *Philadelphia Inquirer*, March 11, 1979, p. 10.

13. Budde, "Business Political Action Committees," p. 19.

14. *Ibid.*, p. 11; Epstein, "Business and Labor," pp. 132-133.

15. Budde, "Business Political Action Committees," p. 21; and Perham, "New Zest of Corporate PACs," p. 50.

16. Fred Radewagen, "Organization of a Political Action Committee," in *Guidelines for Corporate Political Action Committees*, pp. 6-7.

17. *Ibid.*, p. 11.

18. *Ibid.*, p. 14.

Bibliography

Alexander, Herbert E. *Financing Politics: Money, Elections and Political Reform*. Washington, D.C.: Congressional Quarterly Press, 1976.

_____ . *Financing the 1976 Election*. Washington, D.C.: Congressional Quarterly Press, 1979.

_____ . "The Folklore of Buying Elections." *Business and Society Review*, no. 2 (Summer 1972), pp. 48-53.

_____ . *PACs: What They Are: How They Are Changing Political Campaign Financing Patterns*. Washington, Conn.: The Center for Information on America, 1979.

_____ . *Political Financing*. Minneapolis, Minn.: Burgess Publishing Co., 1972.

_____ . *Money and Politics*. Washington, D.C.: Public Affairs Press, 1972.

An Analysis of the Impact of the Federal Election Campaign Act 1972-1978, a Report by the Campaign Finance Study Group to the Committee on House Administration of the U.S. House of Representatives. Cambridge, Mass.: Institute of Politics, John F. Kennedy School of Government, Harvard University, May 1979.

Bennett, Keith W. "PACs: Staying Afloat on the Washington Scene." *Iron Age*, 2 July 1979, p. 36.

Berlow, Alan, and Weiss, Laura B. "Energy PACs: Potential Power in Elections." *Congressional Quarterly Weekly Report* 37 (1979):2455-61.

Bethell, Tom. "Taking a Hard Look at Common Cause." *New York Times Magazine*, 24 August 1980, p. 34.

Bradford, W. Murray. "How to Get Business Heard in the Political Arena." *Price Waterhouse Review* 23 (1978):12-19.

Bretton, Henry L. *The Power of Money*. Albany, N.Y.: State University of New York Press, 1980.

Buchanan, Christopher. "New Limits on PAC Contributions Advanced." *Congressional Quarterly Weekly Report* 37 (1979):2337-2338.

Buchanan, Christopher. "Obey-Railsback Plan Stalled in the Senate by Threat of Filibuster." *Congressional Quarterly Weekly Report* 38 (1980):33.

Cathey, Paul. "Business Casts Its Vote for Political Activism." *Iron Age*, 7 April 1980, pp. 28-30.

Cohen, David. "The Special Interest Money Flood." *Citizen Participation* 1 (1979):1-12.

Cohen, Richard E. "Congressional Democrats Beware—Here Come the Corporate PACs." *National Journal* 12 (1980):1304-1309.

Cohen, Richard E. "Running Scared in Congress—the Parties Go Head-to-Head Over Money." *National Journal* 10 (1978):557-561

Cook, Rhodes. "Fund Raising Doubles Since Four Years Ago." *Congressional Quarterly Weekly Report* 38 (1980):569-571.

Copeland, G.W. "The Politics of Campaign Finance Reform in Congress—The Story of HR 1." *Legislative Studies Quarterly* 6 (1981):141-151.

Dupuy, William L. "The Political Action Committee and the Public Relations Practitioner." *Public Relations Quarterly* 26 (1981):14-16.

Edwards, H.L. "Grass Roots Politics and Political Action Committees." *Mining Congress Journal* 63 (1977):34-38.

Elliott, L.A. "You Can't Judge PACs by the Numbers Alone." *Association Management* 32 (1980):167-169.

Epstein, Edwin M. "The Business PAC Phenomenon: An Irony of Electoral Reform." *Regulation* 3 (1979):35-41.

———. "Corporations and Labor Unions in Electoral Politics." *The Annals of the American Academy of Political and Social Science* 425 (1976):33-58.

———. "Dimensions of Corporate Power." In *Selected Major Issues in Business' Role in Modern Society,* edited by George A. Steiner, Los Angeles, Calif.: Graduate School of Management, U.C.L.A., 1973, pp. 269-357.

———. "The Emergence of Political Action Committees." In *Political Finance,* Sage Electoral Studies Yearbook, vol. 5, edited by Herbert E. Alexander, Beverly Hills, Calif.: Sage Publications, 1979, pp. 159-197.

Fanelli, J.J. "Political Action Committees." *The Corporate Director* 1 (1980):14-18.

Farney, Dennis. "Harnessing the PAC Bomb." *Wall Street Journal,* 4 December 1978, p. 26.

Glen, Maxwell. "At the Wire, Corporate PACs Come through for the GOP." *National Journal* 11 (1979):174-177.

———. "Liberal Political Action Committees Borrow a Page from the Conservatives." *National Journal* 13 (1981):1197-1200.

———. "The PACs are Back, Richer and Wiser, to Finance the 1980 Elections." *National Journal* 11 (1979):1982-1984.

Golden, L. "A Dangerous Rush to Political Action." *Business Week,* 25 September 1978, p. 14.

Haas, Lynn Swann. "Taking Political Action." *Dallas Magazine* 59 (1980), p. 67.

Handler, Edward; Mulkern, John R.; and Godfredsen, Lawrence. "Diversity and Cohesion in Corporate Political Behavior: A Micro-Analysis of the Campaign Contribution Strategies of Corporate Political Action Committees." *Proceeding of the 40th Annual Meeting of the Academy of Management.* Detroit, Michigan: 9-13 August 1980, pp. 361-365.

Heard, Alexander. *The Costs of Democracy.* Chapel Hill, N.C.: The University of North Carolina Press, 1962.

Hucker, Charles W. "Corporate Political Action Committees Are Less Oriented to Republicans Than Expected." *Congressional Quarterly Weekly Report* 36 (1978):849-854.

Jacobson, Gary C. *Money in Congressional Elections.* New Haven, Conn.: Yale University Press, 1980.

Katskee, Melvin R. "PACs: Should National Banks Stay Away?" *Banking Law Journal* 96 (1979):738-745.

Keim, Gerald D. "Foundations of a Political Strategy for Business." *California Management Review* 23 (1981):41-48.

Kimball, Thomas L. "Examining Corporate Influence: A Pressing National Priority." *National Wildlife* 18 (1980), p. 28.

Kirschten, Dick. "Corporate PACs—The GOP's Ace in the Hole?" *National Journal* 10 (1978):1899-1902.

Kroger, William. "Business PACs are Coming of Age." *Nation's Business* 66 (1978):38-41.

Lewis, Ephraim. "A Liberal Attack on PACs." *Business Week,* 25 December 1978, p. 185.

Light, Larry. "Business Giving Heavily to GOP." *Congressional Quarterly Weekly Report* 38 (1980):3405-3409.

Lindblom, Charles E. *Politics and Markets.* New York: Basic Books, 1977.

McGrath, Phyllis S. *Redefining Corporate-Federal Relations.* New York: Conference Board, 1979.

Malbin, Michael J. "Campaign Financing and the Special Interests." *Public Interest* 56 (1979):21-42.

———. "Labor, Business, and Money—A Post Election Analysis." *National Journal* 9 (1977):416-417.

———, ed. *Parties, Interest Groups, and Campaign Finance Laws.* Washington, D.C.: American Enterprise Institute for Public Policy Research, 1980.

Matasar, Ann B. "Corporate Responsibility Gone Awry? The Corporate Political Action Committee." Prepared for delivery at the 1981 Annual Meeting of the American Political Science Association, 3 September 1981.

Mayton, William T. "Nixon's PACs Americana." *Washington Monthly* 11 (1980), p. 54.

McDonald, Kimberly. "The Impact of Political Action Committees on the American Electoral Process." *Economic Forum* 12 (1981):94-103.

Miller, William H. "The New Clout of Corporate PACs." *Industry Week* 207 (1980), p. 115.

Mulkern, John R.; Handler, Edward; and Godtfredsen, Lawrence. "Corporate PACs as Fundraisers." *California Management Review* 23 (1981):49-55.

North, James. "The Politics of Selfishness." *The Washington Monthly* 10 (1978):32-36.

Obey, David R.; Frenzel, Bill; Railsback, Thomas F.; and Bauman, Robert E. "Is the House-Passed Act to Limit Nonparty Political Committee Contributions Sound?" *Congressional Digest* 58 (1979), p. 308.

Perham, John C. "Big Year for Company Political Action." *Dun's Review* 111 (1978):100-102.

———. "Capitalism Comes Out of the Closet." *Dun's Review* 107 (1976):47-49.

———. "The New Zest of the Corporate PACs." *Dun's Review* 115 (1980):50-52.

Pigott, Richard J.; and Williamson, Richard S. "Corporate Political Activity." *Business Lawyer* 34 (1979):913-919.

Quigley, Fred K., Jr. "Employee Political Involvement." *Public Relations Journal* 12 (1976):16-18.

Radewagen, Fred. *Guidelines for Political Action Committees.* Washington, D.C.: U.S. Chamber of Commerce, 1977.

Roeder, Edward. "Catalyzing Favorable Reactions: A Look at Chemical Industry PACs." *Sierra Club Bulletin* 66 (1981), p. 23.

Rosen, Gerald R. "Corporate PACs Under Fire." *Dun's Review* 117 (1981), p. 5.

Sansweet, Stephen J. "PAC Pressure? Political Action Units at Firms are Assailed by Some Over Tactics." *Wall Street Journal,* 24 July 1980, p. 1.

Scribner, Tom, ed. "Symposium: Political Action Committees and Campaign Finance." *Arizona Law Review* 22 (1980):351-674.

Sethi, S. Prakash. "Serving the Public Interest: Corporate Political Action Strategies in the 1980's." *Management Review* 70 (1981):8-11.

Swanson, Carl L. "Corporations and Electoral Activities: The Legal, Political, and Managerial Implications of PACs." In *Private Enterprise and Public Purpose,* eds. S. Prakash Sethi and Carl L. Swanson, pp. 355-372. New York: John Wiley & Sons, Inc., 1981.

Tumin, Jonathan. "How to Bury Liberals, (Conservative Money Offensive.)" *New Republic,* 24 May 1980, p. 13.

U.S. Congress, Committee on House Administration, *Public Financing of Congressional Elections: Hearings on H.R. 1.,* 96th Congress, 1st sess. 15-27 March 1979.

Weinberger, Marvin I.; and Greevy, Dave. *The PAC Directory.* Cambridge, Mass.: Ballinger Publishing Co., 1981.

Weidenbaum, Murray L. "Public Policy: No Longer a Spectator Sport for Business." *Journal of Business Strategy* 1 (1980):46-53.

Wertheimer, Fred. "Has Congress Made It Legal to Buy Congressmen?" *Business and Society Review,* no. 27 (Fall 1978), pp. 29-32.

Wertheimer, Fred; and Dart, Justin. "Keep Business Cash Out of Politics?" *U.S. News and World Report,* 30 April 1979, p. 53.

Zippo, Mary. "Politics and Work: Do They Mix?" *Personnel* 58 (1981):43-44.

Index

Railroads, 28, 102-103, 106
Reagan, Ronald, 8
Regulatory agencies, 31
Regulatory environments, 29-32
Reporting practice, 89-94
Republican National Committee, 99
Retailing industry, 65

Sample, 4-5
Solicitation, 43-54; methods and guide-
    lines, 43-46

Split giving, 84-89
Stockholders, 38-42
Sun-PAC opinion, 38, 42, 60

Transportation sector, 28
Trustee plans, 58
Twice-yearly option, 42-43

Vanderjagt (H.R. Republican), 8
Voluntarism, 109

Whyte, William, 54

About the Authors

Edward Handler, professor of government at Babson College, is the author of four books: *Problems in Labor Legislation* (1956), *Small Business and Pattern Bargaining* (1961), *America and Europe in the Political Thought of John Adams* (1964), and *The American Political Experience* (1968). He received the A.B., M.A., and Ph.D. degrees from Harvard University. He teaches undergraduate courses in corporate power and responsibility and current American foreign policy and a graduate course in business and society. He was chairman of Babson College's Liberal Arts Division and currently chairs its Board of Research.

John R. Mulkern, associate professor of history at Babson College, received the A.B. from Northeastern University, the M.A. from the University of Florida, and the Ph.D. from Boston University. He was formerly on the faculty at Boston State College, Northeastern University, Cushing College, and Emerson College. Professor Mulkern is the author of a number of articles on American politics. He teaches courses in American history and American politics.